POGGIO
CIVITATE
(MURLO)

Cities and Communities of the Etruscans

NANCY THOMSON DE GRUMMOND AND
LISA C. PIERACCINI, SERIES EDITORS

This series was initiated to open discussion and ask questions about what defines an Etruscan city. How did Etruscan cities arise, and what can they tell us about urbanism in ancient Italy? How did Etruscan cities create their own identities, and how are they similar to or different from each other? These queries can be applied to the study of the "Twelve Peoples of the Etruscans," a conventional historical term used in ancient Rome to refer to the most important cities of the Etruscans, the majority of which can be identified today. The aim of this book series is to stimulate and contribute to current vigorous debates concerning Etruscan culture and art, state formation, urban development, and the socioeconomic characteristics of settlements in Etruria.

To understand the major Etruscan cities better, it is also vital to look at the numerous smaller settlements and discuss their similarities to and differences from one another and the larger cities nearby. How can we trace how Etruscan communities developed differently from cities? Did these settlements play a distinctive role in networks of trade in comparison to the large cities? Did smaller communities produce the same arts as their sizable neighbors? Did they worship different Etruscan gods from those of the great cities?

By asking such questions we hope to access the social, religious, economic, architectural, artistic, and civic fabric of each Etruscan city and community. This approach highlights the unique Etruscan contributions to ancient Italy without relying heavily on the traditional methodologies that look to Greece or Rome to explain Etruscan customs, culture, art, and traditions.

POGGIO CIVITATE (MURLO)

ANTHONY TUCK

University of Texas Press

AUSTIN

This book has been supported by an endowment dedicated to
classics and the ancient world and funded by the Areté Foundation;
the James R. Dougherty, Jr. Foundation; the Rachael and Ben Vaughan
Foundation; and the National Endowment for the Humanities.

Requests for permission to reproduce material from this work should be sent to:
Permissions
University of Texas Press
P.O. Box 7819
Austin, TX 78713-7819
utpress.utexas.edu/rp-form

♾ The paper used in this book meets the minimum requirements
of ANSI/NISO Z39.48-1992 (R1997) (Permanence of Paper).

Library of Congress Cataloging-in-Publication Data

Names: Tuck, Anthony, author.
Title: Poggio Civitate (Murlo) / Anthony Tuck.
Other titles: Cities and communities of the Etruscans.
Description: First edition. | Austin : University of Texas Press,
2021. | Series: Cities and communities of the Etruscans |
Includes bibliographical references and index.
Identifiers: LCCN 2020047100
ISBN 978-1-4773-2294-9 (cloth)
ISBN 978-1-4773-2295-6 (paperback)
ISBN 978-1-4773-2296-3 (library ebook)
ISBN 978-1-4773-2297-0 (nonlibrary ebook)
Subjects: LCSH: Architecture, Domestic—Italy—Poggio Civitate Site. |
Decoration and ornament, Architectural—Italy—Poggio Civitate Site. |
Industries—Italy—Poggio Civitate Site. | Poggio Civitate Site (Italy)
Classification: LCC DG70.P64 T835 2021 | DDC 937/.566—dc23
LC record available at https://lccn.loc.gov/2020047100

doi:10.7560/322949

CONTENTS

ILLUSTRATIONS

ACKNOWLEDGMENTS

The longevity and success of the Poggio Civitate Archaeological Project are a testament to the hundreds of people who have lent it their energy, talent, creativity, and passion. Every summer since 1966, students have come to Murlo to work and learn with a community of equally passionate citizens as together they explore a shared past. Generations of scholars from the Soprintendenza Archeologia, Belle Arti e Paesaggio di Firenze and the Soprintendenza Archeologia, Belle Arti e Paesaggio per le province di Siena, Grosseto e Arezzo saw fit to bestow upon the project the enormous responsibilities of excavating, recording, and studying this remarkably rich archaeological site. The author would like to specifically thank Silvia Goggioli, Elena Sorge, Irma della Giovampaola, and Jacopo Tabolli for sharing their wisdom over the years. These efforts, six decades in the making, embody the patience and cooperation that can exist among people bound together by a desire to illuminate the past and share it with the world.

First and foremost, the author of this work owes an unpayable debt to his predecessors who served as Director of Excavations at Poggio Civitate: Kyle Meredith Phillips, Jr., and Erik O. Nielsen. These two visionary archaeologists built a program of remarkable strength that continues to thrive. Both Phillips and Nielsen owe their program's success to the incredible teams of students and scholars with whom they worked. Poggio Civitate's current director, the author of this volume, is equally indebted to a great number of people whose professionalism and commitment to the project and the place are boundless. Kate Kreindler, Steven Miller, Jason Bauer, Eoin O'Donoghue, Ann Glennie, Nora Donoghue, Katherine Daley, Ed Clarke, Sarah Kansa, Eric Kansa, Rex Wallace, Jevon Brunk, Taylor Oshan, and Cole Reilly are just a few of the many whose efforts in the field, in the laboratory, and through the digital organization of a vast data archive continue the demanding tradition of excellence established by our predecessors. None of our work would be possible without the support of the University of Massachusetts Amherst Department of Classics and College of Humanities and Fine Arts.

Our efforts often involve the translation of data into images that help communicate our larger interpretive narratives. Another facet of our work over the years involves the creation of a body of visual documentation that allows us to present the material landscape of Poggio Civitate. The photographic archive of the site is an extensive and invaluable resource for illustrating the story of Poggio Civitate. The photographs included in this volume are largely the work of Grayson Lauffenburger and Robert Nisbet, two exceptional photographers among generations who have contributed to our work. Excavation architect Hans Linden's original hand-drawn state plan grew over the years under the direction of David Peck, Goran Soderberg, Greg Kil, Craig Copeland, and Jon Lannan. That plan was converted by Jon Lannan and Aristide Lex into a digital document that grows in both detail and technological complexity with every year. Illustrators led by Ellen Neilsen, Joe McKendry, Evan Batson, Ida Floreak, and especially Jean Blackburn and her teams of talented students have contributed images drawn from argument and imagination to show how life at Poggio Civitate might have once looked.

Special thanks are also owed to Nancy de Grummond and Lisa Pieraccini for their work in making this series of studies on Etruscan cities and communities a reality. Their keen insight and editorial instincts, along with those of Jim Burr, Sarah McGavick, and the remarkable staff of the University of Texas Press were essential to the development and editing of this work. Thanks go as well to the reviewers for their excellent suggestions for revision and improvement. Additionally, Michele Kunitz was especially helpful in reading drafts of this work and providing direction to improve its form and clarity. Lynne Ferguson, Kerri Cox Sullivan, and Sue Gaines provided the critical support needed to bring the project to fruition.

Of course, our work at Poggio Civitate would simply not be possible without the welcoming generosity of generations of friends of the *comune* of Murlo. The author is particularly grateful for the way the town has welcomed his very patient family year after year. The Rubegni family, the Muzzi family, Pablo Fiaschi, Renza Fantone, and so many others have embraced our work and our members for years. We could never hope to repay our debt to them in full, but look forward to many more years of trying, over strong coffee, brilliant food, and sublime wine, and during conversations that stretch on into the smallest hours of the morning.

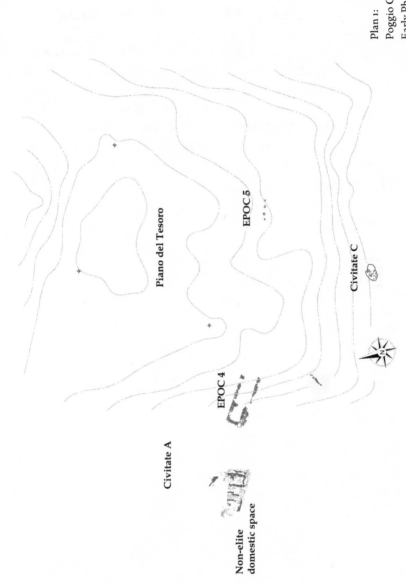

Non-elite
domestic space

Civitate A

EPOC 4

Piano del Tesoro

EPOC 5

Civitate C

N

Plan 1:
Poggio Civitate,
Early Phase

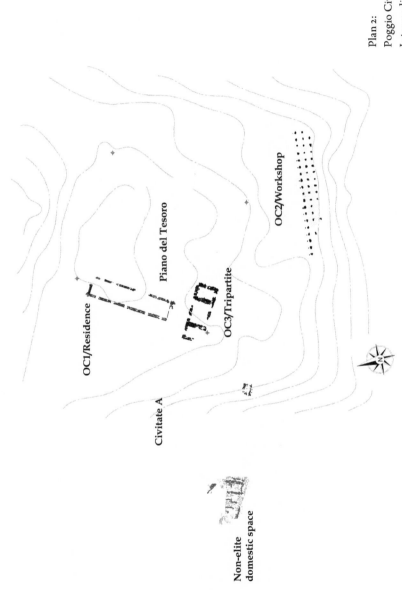

OC1/Residence

Piano del Tesoro

Civitate A

OC3/Tripartite

OC2/Workshop

Non-elite
domestic space

N

Plan 2:
Poggio Civitate,
Intermediate Phase

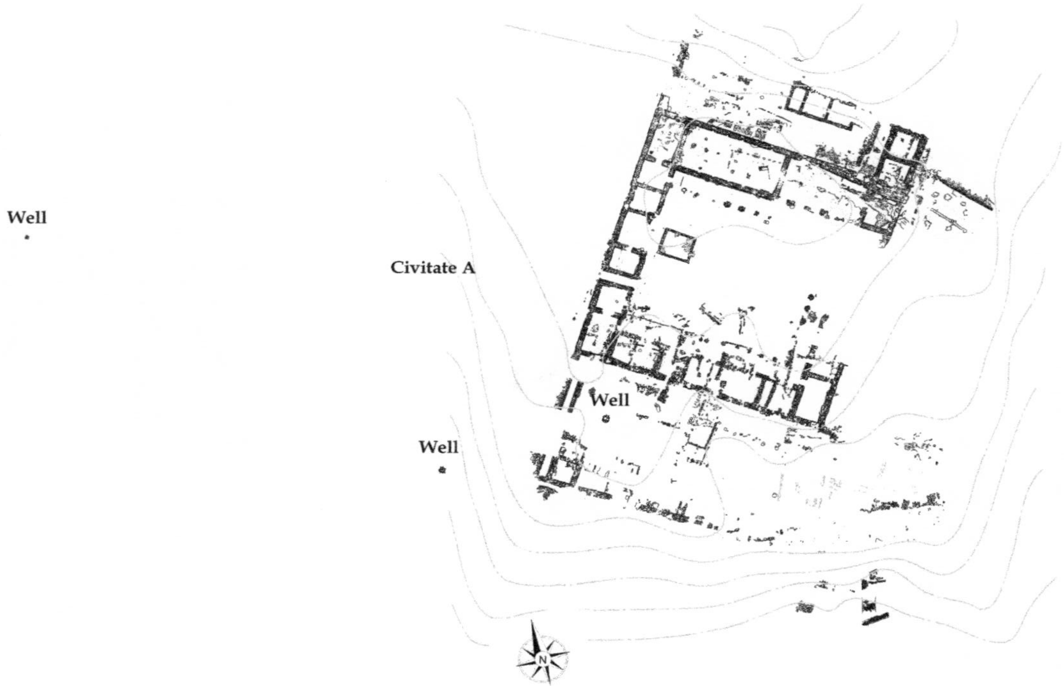

Plan 3:
Poggio Civitate,
Archaic Phase

Civitate A

Well

Well

Well

POGGIO
CIVITATE
(MURLO)

1.1. Map of Tuscany

⊙ 1 ⊙
Introduction

Poggio Civitate is a wooded hilltop straddling the boundary between Tuscany's metal-rich region, known as the Colline Metallifere, to the west and, to the east, the rolling hills of the Crete Senesi, which eventually reach the Apennine foothills (fig. 1.2). The hill stands immediately to the southeast of the walled, medieval community of Murlo.

The name Poggio Civitate is a curious one for an area covered in dense forest at the edge of Tuscany's Maremma region. It appears in Sienese property documents as early as the fourteenth century CE, where it is called Le Civitate.[1] More puzzling still, this name for an unoccupied hilltop is derived from the Latin nominative plural *civitates*. As a result, Poggio Civitate was for centuries an uninhabited, impenetrable forest known as "The Cities." Adding to this mystery are the local references to the hill as "Civita Magna" (Great City) and to a specific plateau near the hill's center as "Piano del Tesoro" (Plateau of the Treasure), all highlighting tenacious local memories of the place's past significance. When the legendary Etruscan archaeologist Ranucchio Bianchi Bandinelli visited the area, locals were glad to show him examples of a range of antiquities casually collected on the hilltop over the years, further hinting at the presence of an ancient community there.[2]

Not until excavation began in 1966 did the reason for these unusual and suggestive toponyms become clear. Poggio Civitate had been the site of a flourishing community in the years between the

1.2. Poggio Civitate from the north

eighth and the late sixth centuries BCE. However, the form of that community was initially a puzzling one to many observers. Monumental architecture on a scale previously unseen in the region once graced the hilltop. Those buildings were ornamented with strange and evocative decorative sculpted figures, all fashioned in local terracotta. More perplexing still was the evidence for the site's ultimate destruction and abandonment. At some point near the end of the sixth century BCE, the community's monumental architecture was torn down in a singular and violent event: the once-proud images of the community's ancestry smashed and their fragments buried, wells and other sources of water filled with architectural debris. The site was thereafter abandoned.

Today, after more than six decades of continuous excavation and exploration, we can see the community of Poggio Civitate with remarkable clarity. During its existence, the leaders of this community engaged in large-scale building projects resulting in some of the most impressive monumental architecture of the early Etruscan period yet known in the region. To realize these projects, Poggio Civitate's population needed to be organized and marshaled by a range of social and economic means, many of which are reflected in the surviving material environment of the site.

The Site and Its Surroundings

Poggio Civitate straddles important geological features of this region of Tuscany. The hill itself sits on the western side of the Siena Basin between the Ombrone River and its tributary, the Crevole, forming the Murlo Ridge.[3] To the west are the hills of the Colline Metallifere, a topographically varied area extending down to the Tuscan coast, geologically consisting of pre-Neogene bedrock. As their name implies, these hills represent a considerable resource of metal ores, especially copper and iron. East of Poggio Civitate is the undulating, gentler topography of the Crete Senesi, a Pleistocene deposit of marine sedimentation geologically called the Siena Basin.[4] Today, the arable lands of the Siena Basin are intensively farmed to produce a range of traditional Tuscan crops. Assuming the area was similarly exploited in antiquity, these paired resources—metals to the west and agriculture to the east, coupled with a defensible, elevated plateau with a high water table—made Poggio Civitate an ideal locale for human occupation.

Most of what is known about communities throughout the region of the Maremma and Crete Senesi comes from evidence gathered in cemeteries. While excavation of Poggio Civitate's necropolis has yielded some information about the funerary behaviors associated with the community, the site also allows comparison of that funerary material to evidence gathered from the spaces where these very same people engaged in the quotidian experiences of their lives. As a result, Poggio Civitate permits us to consider the objects that the community owned and used as well as the spaces where those commodities were manufactured; at times it yields remarkably intimate and poignant traces of the people engaged in the settlement's industry. At Poggio Civitate, we can see and compare the domestic spaces of Etruria's elite aristocracy to those of members of the community's subordinate classes. The site's material remains illustrate religious and narrative ideologies that can serve as guides to navigate the complexities of these social relationships. We can even see evidence of the behaviors of the community toward Poggio Civitate's least empowered people: the remains of infants, who were either stillborn or died within the first few hours or days of life, were recovered not from the community's cemetery but instead from rubbish areas around the community.

The hill's most gradual ascent is from the east. The Ombrone River, running to the southeast of Poggio Civitate, is accessible by means of a path of beaten earth that traverses the spine of Poggio Civitate and terminates at the hill's western extent, a spur known as Poggio Aguzzo. Exploration of Poggio Aguzzo reveals that it served as a necropolis for the people of Poggio Civitate, although other areas of burial may have also been used by varying elements of the community at different points in time.

At approximately the midpoint of Poggio Civitate's east–west axis and immediately north of the path that traverses it is Piano del Tesoro. Extending to the west beyond the plateau is the broad, northerly facing flank of the hilltop. The current state of evidence suggests that the ancient community was concentrated atop these areas, although the dense forest makes wide exploration of areas to the east and south challenging.

Ancient and Medieval History

What follows in this volume is a description of the major phases of Poggio Civitate's community as it developed throughout the Etruscan Orientalizing and Archaic periods.[5] The current state of archaeological evidence at Poggio Civitate conforms to three major phases of architectural development at the site. Each is characterized by an elite habitation of considerable opulence and scale, surrounded by indications of several different areas of non-elite habitation and activity.

The earliest evidence for permanent habitation on the hill dates to the mid-eighth through early seventh centuries BCE. It is possible that subsequent development atop Piano del Tesoro obliterated traces of early activity on the plateau, but evidence of this earliest phase of life at the site is primarily found below the plateau to the south and west. Indications of a curvilinear hut, as well as sporadic recovery of examples of bronze and ceramic types characteristic of the Etruscan Iron Age found throughout this area, hint at permanent habitation.

Either this early population remains largely archaeologically invisible or population dramatically rises at the end of the eighth or the beginning of the seventh century BCE (plan 1). Indications of small houses supported by relatively gracile foundations were located immediately west of Piano del Tesoro along the southern edge of the Civitate A area. These small houses stood to the southwest of a building today called Early Phase Orientalizing Complex Building 4—or EPOC4. EPOC4 was dramatically larger than the small houses below it to the southwest. Moreover, the current state of evidence indicates that the building incorporated novel architectural technologies to support a decorated roof made of terracotta tiles. Traces were found of another structure, perhaps also bearing a roof of terracotta tiles, that appears to have stood several meters to the east, atop Piano del Tesoro; this is referred to as Early Phase Orientalizing Complex Building 5 (EPOC5), although this structure is not well preserved.

EPOC4, EPOC5, and the small houses of the Civitate A area suggest that an early settlement on Poggio Civitate already embodied aspects of the social differentiation that would typify the community throughout its life. The domestic spaces of the community's leaders remained dramatically larger than those of the non-elite families. Moreover, those elite domiciles were used as canvases upon which the emerging iconography of divinely sanctioned leadership was drawn. Aspects of industry present at the site appear to be inwardly directed to satisfy local needs with only token material contact with production systems beyond the community.

Within the second quarter to the middle of the seventh century BCE, the architecture associated with elite activity at Poggio

Civitate is moved to the east and dominates Piano del Tesoro for approximately a century (plan 2). Three structures, each employing a complex and highly ornamental roofing system, occupied three sides of the plateau. Along the plateau's western edge, the community's builders placed a large residence, Orientalizing Complex Building 1/Residence (OC1/Residence). The occupants of this building enjoyed a life of considerable material comfort, at least in comparison to the remains of the still-occupied non-elite houses of the Civitate A area. South of this domicile was a building having a tripartite interior design, Orientalizing Complex Building 3/Tripartite (OC3/Tripartite). Evidence associated with this structure strongly suggests it served some religious purpose. Finally, an industrial center of considerable size was placed along the southeastern edge of the plateau, Orientalizing Complex Building 2/Workshop (OC2/Workshop).

These three buildings were destroyed by fire at the end of the seventh century or in the early years of the sixth century BCE. Replacing them was a structure of impressive size, with an array of enigmatic, evocative sculptures adorning its roof (plan 3). The building consisted of four wings surrounding a partially colonnaded courtyard. At some point after the building's initial construction, defensive works to the southwest and northeast were added. However, these proved ineffective as violence ultimately consumed the community during the later years of the sixth century BCE. The circumstances surrounding the abandonment of Poggio Civitate are among the most enigmatic of the site's many mysteries. The rooftop sculptures were removed and smashed, and their fragments thrown out or buried around the building's perimeter. The wells and water sources were filled in with debris while the walls of the massive building atop Piano del Tesoro were knocked down. From that point onward, the hill remained almost entirely uninhabited.

In the Etruscan period Poggio Civitate was not an isolated settlement within its broader landscape. Traces of other ancient communities have been located on hilltops gracing the same geological divide between the Colline Metallifere and the Crete Senesi,

1.3. View of Murlo from Poggio Civitate

along the north–south border of these two geological features. The resulting picture has the site at Poggio Civitate serving as the political, economic, religious, and social nexus of a nonnuclear community. In fact, the medieval town of Murlo, immediately adjacent to Poggio Civitate, today still acts as the notional center of a number of politically and socially connected communities and may provide a useful model for understanding Poggio Civitate's similar role in antiquity.

Murlo's current form appeared in the twelfth century CE, when the Bishop of Siena built a palazzo in the center of the small, walled community (fig. 1.3).[6] The palazzo still stands above the village, visible from vantage points throughout the area. Communities today, most of which are considerably larger than Murlo itself—and in a reflection of the original, medieval importance of the town—recognize it as the political epicenter of a *comune* of municipally interconnected settlements. Vescovado di Murlo, Casciano di Murlo, La Befa di Murlo, Lumpompesi di Murlo, and several others are all geophysically separate areas of occupation sharing common political and municipal resources and bound together by a shared definition of their community. This commonality is also reflected in a shared modern municipal iconography, which utilizes the image of one of the site's most famous sculptural types, the Poggio Civitate "Cowboy." These figures, wearing wide-brimmed hats, once adorned the roof of the massive edifice that stood during the site's final phase of life. Remarkably, the likely ancient purpose of those evocative images has been fulfilled again: they lend a sense of common cause and shared identity to the modern *comune* of Murlo, just as they once did for the people of Poggio Civitate.

Poggio Civitate before Excavation Began in 1966

Local knowledge of the ancient significance of Poggio Civitate was not limited to the hill's curious name. In 1925, Ranucchio Bianchi Bandinelli traveled to Murlo and was presented with a number of objects supposedly collected in the vicinity of Poggio Civitate and its associated necropolis, Poggio Aguzzo.[7] These materials survive and are on display in the Murlo Antiquarium. Several are suggestive of wealthy burials, from which they likely were casually or intentionally looted over time. An example is the two similar bronze and iron belt buckles that were among this group. The buckles consist of two square elements within which is placed an openwork representation of a stag. Around the squared perimeter are crescent-shaped iron inlays (fig. 1.4). A bronze Negau-style helmet with small finials in the form of palmettes was also among these materials (fig. 1.5).[8] Recent rescue excavation in the nearby community of Grotti at the western edge of the *comune* of Murlo recovered items from the burial of a warrior with whom was interred a nearly identical helmet.

In the mid-1960s, American archaeologist Kyle Meredith Phillips Jr. sought to explore an Etruscan settlement in the region. Phillips was keenly aware that much of what was then known of the Etruscans was the result of excavation of cemeteries. While the images of Tarquinia's painted tombs or the spectacular remains of elite burials from Caere, Vetulonia, and Chiusi had certainly shaped modern

1.4. Bronze and iron belt buckle from Poggio Aguzzo

1.5. Bronze Negau-style helmet

1.6. Poggio Civitate in 1966 prior to excavations

appreciation of these people, Phillips sought evidence of daily life as a way to better understand the communities and the people who created the remarkable materials invested in their burials. Phillips approached Bianchi Bandinelli, then the Superintendent responsible for the archaeological heritage of the region around Florence. Phillips' vision of exploring the lived experience of Etruscan communities resonated with Bianchi Bandinelli's memory of his time in Murlo and the oddly named hill beside the medieval town. At Bianchi Bandinelli's suggestion, exploration of Poggio Civitate would begin. Phillips and his team began work on the hill in 1966, setting in motion a tradition of revelation and discovery that continues to this day.

While evidence for Poggio Civitate's form prior to excavation is limited, archival photographs indicate that the western flank of the Piano del Tesoro plateau was once demarcated by an elongated mound (fig. 1.6).[9] Initial speculation concerning this mound suggested it served as a defensive *agger*, but subsequent consideration showed the mound was more likely a result of the collapsed wall and roofing of the Archaic Phase Building's western wing. During that initial season, exploration of the northern and southern edges of the plateau revealed traces of architecture that were described as Complex 1 and Complex 2. As seasons of excavation progressed, it was revealed that these apparently separate structures were in fact wings of the same building. However, this initial error is entirely understandable. No structure of this form or scale had hitherto been seen in central Italy.

In this and many other ways, the steady progress of excavation and discovery at Poggio Civitate has contributed to an evolving understanding of the site and its surroundings. The evidence it has produced illuminates as frequently as it confounds, revealing its secrets in both mundane and surprising ways. What follows is a synthesis of a great many ideas and arguments offered by the generations of scholars who have studied Poggio Civitate. Like all archaeological inquiry, however, the narrative is only as current as the next season of discovery.

◦ 2 ◦
The Earliest Community of Poggio Civitate

*(Late Eighth Century BCE to the First Quarter/
Middle of the Seventh Century BCE)*

Unlike many examples of emerging urban centers elsewhere in Etruria, Poggio Civitate so far does not preserve significant evidence of occupation dating to earlier than the mid to late eighth century BCE. Sporadic recovery of elements of coil-made pottery, and scattered examples of early types of ornamental bronzes such as fibulae, suggest a degree of limited activity on the hill throughout the Iron Age. However, by the late eighth or early seventh century BCE, available evidence does suggest a permanent community atop the hill.

Domestic activity of this period is preserved in only a few parts of the site. One such area is located immediately south of the southern edge of the Piano del Tesoro plateau and at a considerably lower elevation. This portion of Poggio Civitate is known locally as Civitatine and is now referred to as Civitate C. The evidence from this area indicates the presence of a curvilinear hut (CC7 Hut), represented by an oval depression, cut into the dense clay, with dimensions of approximately 5 by 7 meters. Preserved indications of postholes suggest a timbered frame surrounding a nominally countersunk floor (fig. 2.1).

While occasional concentrations of carbon and charcoal were encountered during the excavation of this feature, the volume and concentration were insufficient to justify the assertion that the structure was destroyed by fire. Instead, excavators believe the building was dismantled or simply abandoned, and afterward the depressed

2.1. Aerial view of the CC7 Hut

area of the building's floor was used as a refuse midden. The range of debris recovered from this depression reflects both domestic and industrial activities dating to the years between the late eighth and approximately the second quarter of the seventh century BCE. This time span is reflected by the datable materials recovered within the midden, none of which can be assigned to a point in time later than the second quarter of the seventh century BCE.[1]

Some of the materials recovered from within this midden may be associated with manufacturing at either a household or a larger scale. Certain features of the deposit also hint at aspects of industry connected to the social and political identity of the site's emerging aristocracy. As would be expected from a domestic space, spindle whorls, loom weights, and rocchetti (ceramic spool-like objects used for various types of textile production) were recovered in considerable concentration. An unusually large proportion of ceramics found within the depression consisted of finer, often ornamented forms; these were especially remarkable in comparison to the ce-

2.2. Murex shells from the midden in the CC7 Hut

ramic assemblages recovered in the environs of the simple houses of a slightly later date excavated to the west.

Most curiously, excavators recovered hundreds of specimens of a specific species of murex shell, the *Bolinus brandaris*.[2] In total, more than one thousand specimens of this mollusk were recovered, grouped in a localized, concentrated area within the depression (fig. 2.2). *Bolinus brandaris* are native to the central and western Mediterranean, so their presence at Poggio Civitate would have required them to be transported a distance of about 70 kilometers up the Ombrone River from the coast. The specimens could be connected to food preparation, which is also reflected in the quantities of butchered bone found nearby.[3] However, absent means of live transportation or preservation, it seems unlikely that these animals could have been easily brought from the ocean for local consumption. Moreover, every specimen recovered within the depression was broken. This suggests the much greater likelihood that the mollusks were collected and brought to Poggio Civitate for purposes for which they were justly famous in antiquity: dye production.[4] This species of mollusk produced a reddish-purple dye used in textile production, and those purplish hues demonstrated high social status and rank in the later Etruscan and Roman periods.[5]

The presence of these particular mollusks coupled with abundant evidence of fiber spinning and textile production recovered in the immediate vicinity hints at the possibility that features of the visual and material signals associated with the broader Italic traditions of elite social rank were forming at Poggio Civitate even at this early date.

Early Phase Orientalizing Complex Building 4 (EPOC4)

During the years between the end of the eighth century and the first half of the seventh BCE, laborers constructed a building of then-unprecedented technological form and scale for the community, referred to by the excavators as EPOC4 (fig. 2.3). The building was a large, rectangular structure oriented on an east–west axis with the eastern end open. It had a wide stone foundation that extended 20.5 m along its east–west axis, with a width of 7.6 m. The porch employed an internal dimension of 12.8 by 5.7 m. Its open eastern end was oriented to the rising sun, allowing both visibility

2.3. Aerial view of EPOC4 from the southwest

and accessibility. Its back room, measuring approximately 5.35 by 5.1 m, was separated from the porch, creating a somewhat more private space within the structure. EPOC4 is notably similar in form to examples of structures dated to the first half of the seventh century BCE from the sites of San Giovenale and Roselle, further confirming its likely period of use.[6]

EPOC4's robust foundation walls measure an average of 1.1 m in thickness. While sections of the northern foundation wall were damaged during early years of exploratory excavation, the southern wall is entirely preserved and its length of 20.5 m is noteworthy. As we will see with the later structures on the site, the terracotta roofing tiles employed at Poggio Civitate—pantiles—display some variation in overall length, but are remarkably uniform in width, measuring a consistent 0.54 m. This consistency is understandable. Foundation walls for structures employing terracotta roofs would have needed to be designed in lengths divisible by a whole number of such tiles' widths. Not surprisingly, the dimensions of all of Poggio Civitate's large buildings in its subsequent two phases of development display this even divisibility of length.[7] However, given the comparatively early date of EPOC4, the fact that its length is also divisible by almost exactly forty units of 0.54 m is surprising, as, together with EPOC4's wide foundation walls, it suggests that the building bore such a tiled roof.[8] Moreover, traces of ornamental elements such as horn akroteria and unusual decorative plaques further suggest that the building displayed decorative features consistent with the early iconography of an emerging elite, aristocratic identity.[9]

Materials recovered from EPOC4's floor indicate that the building served as a domestic space, although its large porch area may have hosted other functions. Grains and grape seeds collected from the porch's floor point to food preparation within that space, while a number of spindle whorls and rocchetti indicate that the typical domestic activity of fiber processing and possibly textile production likely occurred here as well (fig. 2.4).

To the southwest of EPOC4, excavation revealed traces of sev-

2.4. Rocchetto from EPOC4 floor

eral smaller structures. The range of similar types of materials—cooking wares and other forms of simple domestic pottery, fiber and textile equipment such as spindle whorls and rocchetti, and a number of other utilitarian objects—indicates that these buildings also served as domiciles. However, the considerably less robust foundations of these buildings suggest they did not support tiled, terracotta roofs.[10] Instead, these narrower foundations would have been suitable for thatch or some other lighter roofing material.

Common types of ceramics recovered from some of these domestic spaces indicate a degree of chronological overlap with EPOC4, although people continued to live in these structures after EPOC4's abandonment and into Poggio Civitate's Intermediate Phase of social and political development. Some of the ceramics recovered from within and around these houses also suggest a degree of overlap with the oval hut described above and located to the southeast of EPOC4 and this cluster of small domiciles. Therefore, it is possible that Poggio Civitate preserves evidence of evolving technological forms associated with different types of domestic architecture of the eighth and early seventh century BCE. Curvilinear huts characteristic of the Etruscan Iron Age may have still stood to the east in the Civitatine area of Poggio Civitate, even as rectilinear architectural forms of similar scale developed in closer proximity to EPOC4. EPOC4—standing at nearly ten times the

2.5. View of possible EPOC5 structure, from the southeast

size of these smaller domestic spaces and employing a tiled, terra-cotta roof—would have been comparatively impressive in scale, presumably representing the domestic space of the growing community's leading family.

The immediate proximity of EPOC4 to these smaller domestic structures may explain why EPOC4 was abandoned at some point in the second quarter of the seventh century BCE. The deep porch of EPOC4 created a semi-public space, perhaps used for gatherings or periodic collective meals. However, the absence of an eastern wall would have also permitted constant visibility of the activities occurring within that space. As Poggio Civitate and the surrounding region developed a system of political and social organization driven by ideologies of aristocratic familial identity and inheritance, members of this social elite grew increasingly interested in restricting visible access to their daily experience.[11] As a result, at some point in the second quarter of the seventh century BCE EPOC4 was abandoned. It is equally likely that after its abandonment its salvageable building materials, such as roof tiles and wooden timbers, were stripped away and reused elsewhere, perhaps in the construction of buildings of the site's Intermediate Phase.[12] At this point we see the clear emergence of Poggio Civitate's governing ideology, complete with a series of buildings designed at a scale to compete with anything else known throughout the region.

Early Phase Orientalizing Complex Building 5 (EPOC5)

Traces of a building that may be contemporary with EPOC4 were identified several meters to the east of EPOC4 atop Piano del Tesoro. Extensive exploration of this area has revealed only a few examples of irregularly shaped, flat stones that appear to be bases for wooden columns (fig. 2.5). The center point of each of these stones is separated from the others by a uniform distance of 2.7 m. As noted above concerning the roof of EPOC4, this spacing's divisibility by units of 0.54 m is strongly suggestive of an architectural intentionality. However, the poorly preserved remains of EPOC5 and the absence of a sufficient body of materials associated with it make confidence on this point impossible.

◦ 3 ◦
The Lords of Piano del Tesoro

THE "ORIENTALIZING PERIOD COMPLEX"

*(ca. 675/650 BCE to the End of the Seventh or
Beginning of the Sixth Century BCE)*

Within or around the years of the second quarter of the seventh century BCE, members of Poggio Civitate's community initiated the construction of a complex of buildings situated at the top of the plateau immediately to the east of the EPOC4 structure (fig. 3.1). Three buildings, each with distinct functions, displayed a common decorative program consisting of "cutout" akroteria attached directly to their ridgepole tiles. Additionally, the lateral gutters of roofs (*simae*) of each building held human-headed antefixes alternating with feline waterspouts. The simae running along the buildings' length would guide and direct water through controlled channels.

All three buildings were impressively large, and stood around an open space that anticipated the courtyard area of Poggio Civitate's final phase of monumental building, to be described below. The best hypotheses for the use of these buildings identify them as a residential structure, a building of sacred or religious nature, and an industrial center. The three buildings stood together atop the plateau at some point in the second half of the seventh century BCE and were destroyed in a single fire that swept across the hilltop around the end of the seventh or beginning of the sixth century BCE.

The Orientalizing Complex
ORIENTALIZING COMPLEX BUILDING 1/ RESIDENCE (OC1/RESIDENCE)

Orientalizing Complex Building 1, conjectured to be a residence, stood on the western edge of the Piano del Tesoro plateau, approximately

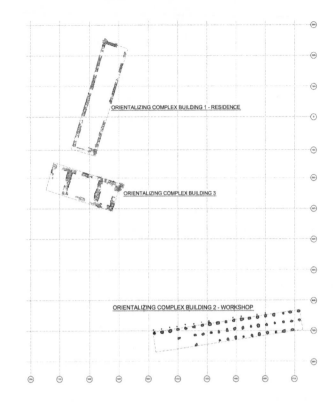

a

ORIENTALIZING COMPLEX BUILDING 1 - RESIDENCE

ORIENTALIZING COMPLEX BUILDING 3

ORIENTALIZING COMPLEX BUILDING 2 - WORKSHOP

b

3.1. Plan (a) and reconstruction (b) of Orientalizing Complex

15 meters from the location of EPOC4. It is not possible to say if the abandonment of EPOC4 occurred prior to, during, or immediately after OC1/Residence's construction. However, it remains clear that over time elite habitation at the site pushed further to the east, away from the cluster of smaller, non-elite houses originally adjacent to EPOC4.

OC1/Residence extended 36.2 m along an approximately north–south axis, with a width of between 8.4 and 8.6 m. Preserved on the building's floor were numerous examples of cooking wares and storage vessels,[1] along with elements of a considerable banquet service of locally produced and imported ceramics and bronze vessels. Furniture and small wooden objects throughout the building were ornamented with a wide array of carved bone and antler inlays and figurines. Cosmetic equipment and a range of personal objects all point to a reasonably elegant material life for the inhabitants of this building.

ORIENTALIZING COMPLEX BUILDING 3/ TRIPARTITE (OC3/TRIPARTITE)

Immediately south of—and perpendicular to—OC1/Residence stood another building contemporary with the residence. Although its foundations were badly damaged, enough was preserved to provide a picture of its original form. OC3/Tripartite, so called because of its three-chambered interior organization, was somewhat shorter in length but wider than OC1/Residence, and employed very robust foundations. Unlike OC1/Residence, the building employed two interior walls to form a tripartite division of space, with the two flanking chambers each having half the area of the central room. In total, the overall plan of OC3/Tripartite reflects a building of 23.5 m in length and 9.2 m in width.

Materials recovered within and around OC3/Tripartite were both considerably more scarce and less indicative of a specific building function than those recovered at OC1/Residence. The building's tripartite division of space, along with examples of highly distinctive ceramics recovered from the preserved portions of the building's floor, suggest that OC3/Tripartite served the religious needs of the site's elite family and the surrounding community.

ORIENTALIZING COMPLEX BUILDING 2/ WORKSHOP (OC2/WORKSHOP)

Positioned at the extreme southern edge of Piano del Tesoro was the third building in this complex, OC2/Workshop. This structure was extraordinarily large given the presumed date of its construction: it was approximately 8 m wide and extended 54 m along an east–west axis. Evidence collected from the floor of the building clearly indicates that it served as an industrial center for the community. The material remains of the building and its environs reflect bronzeworking, bone and antler carving, ceramic and terracotta production, the spinning of fibers, and the processing of foodstuffs.

CONSTRUCTION METHODS

All three Orientalizing Complex buildings had timber superstructures that supported wattle and daub walling. Numerous examples of preserved daub show the woven lattice of wattles and also reveal a number of additional details concerning the timbering of these buildings. For example, one specimen[2] preserves a curved surface: the negative impression of a beam from OC2/Workshop.

Another piece of daub[3] illuminates an aspect of an otherwise problematic feature of OC2/Workshop: that of the building's lateral stability. OC2/Workshop's absence of lateral walls, coupled with the weight of the building's roof, would significantly challenge the building's stability. Moreover, its position at the plateau's edge would have made an unwalled building's roof susceptible to pressure from the updraft of the southerly winds that are characteristic of summer afternoons in the area. In order to lend greater support to the vertical timbers holding up the roof, builders utilized diagonal struts infilled with wattle and daub, presumably at the upper portion of each column's intersection with a horizontal beam. The

3.2. Daub piece from OC2/Workshop

3.3. Reconstruction of wattle and daub element in position

roughly triangular element of daub shown in figure 3.2 preserves indications of horizontally oriented wattles with daub left draping over the reeds through the action of gravity. This orientation means that this specimen could not have filled the triangular area of a gable, as originally supposed by the excavators.[4] Instead, the downward keying of the daub requires that the fragment had been positioned vertically, as presented in figure 3.3, and thus potentially helping to stabilize this element of the roof.

Each building had a terracotta roof consisting of arrangements of pantiles and cover tiles that had been produced using molds. Registers of pantiles were placed upon purlins and rafters, apparently secured only by their own weight.[5] The space between each register was covered with another register of hemicircular cover tiles. The final register of pantiles at the eaves of each building was fronted by a lateral sima wall perforated by a waterspout, while the aperture of the final cover tile was covered with an antefix.[6] The apex of each roof was surmounted by a larger version of the hemicircular tiles that enclosed the ridgepole, given the name "ridgepole tile." Attached to these ridgepole tiles was a range of decorative sculptures, discussed below.[7]

Evidence for the Date of the Orientalizing Complex

Much of our understanding of early Etruscan chronology depends upon the accuracy of dating schemes developed for Greek ceramics. Therefore, it must be stated at the outset of this discussion that any adjustment to the latter will necessarily influence the former.

With that proviso, Greek ceramics recovered from the floor surfaces of all three buildings of this complex provide a very strong indication of the approximate date of the fire that destroyed the structures. Numerous examples of Ionian cups, produced at any number of possible centers along the western coast of modern Turkey, were recovered from the floors of OC1/Residence and OC2/Workshop (fig. 3.4).[8] These cups, which display low, conical bases, wide shoulders, everted rims, and two horizontal loop handles, are

3.4. Ionian cup from OC1/Residence floor

imitated in local bucchero,[9] perhaps explaining their presence in OC2/Workshop, as they may have served as models for local potters. In addition to these Ionian cups, a few examples of Corinthian, Rhodian, Samian, and Chiote banqueting wares and transport amphorae were recovered from the area around OC1/Residence. Current thinking regarding these various Eastern Mediterranean imports places their date of manufacture between the years 620 and 580 BCE.[10]

Determining the date of the construction of the three buildings of the complex is more challenging. From the floor of OC3/Tripartite and the environs of OC2/Workshop, excavation recovered fragments of a specific type of bucchero vessel, a "relief ware" style (fig. 3.5). This class of vessel, which consists primarily of kyathoi (a drinking vessel with a single, vertically oriented

handle)—although some examples of kantharoi (similar to a kyathos but with two vertical handles) are known—typically employs
an unusual style of decoration wherein excess clay is delicately adhered to the interior surface of the vessel's bowl to create relief designs. On some examples of this class of vessel, additional incision
is added to the raised interior surface to enhance the relief design.

Recent scholarship concerning these vessels has identified two
different production centers, each creating slightly different forms
of the class.[11] One form has broad ribbon handles, the surfaces of
which are deeply incised with parallel grooves, and usually has
hemispherical bowls; this style also displays additional incision to
highlight the associated relief decoration. This particular class also
sometimes includes inscriptions naming a person from a specific
family, the *Paithna* or *Paithinaia*, giving the cup to another, un-
named person. The letterforms associated with these inscriptions

3.5. Relief ware bucchero

indicate a southern Etruscan production center, one which most scholars identify as Cerveteri.

The second style of this class of vessel frequently displays a specific and unusual type of handle. The base of this handle is attached to the vessel's exterior wall and extends upward, fanning out into a broad, flat, roughly hourglass-shaped handle. This form of relief ware bucchero vessel is typically slightly smaller than those of the Cerveteri variant. Vessels of this class also sometimes display inscriptions. Unlike those of the Cerveteri class, the letterforms on this type appear to be northern in their epigraphic derivation. However, it is curious and noteworthy that the same *Paithna* or *Paithinaia* family identifies itself as the source of these cups as well; the implications of this are explored below. There is less agreement as to the location of the production center of this second class of relief ware bucchero, although Vetulonia or Populonia have both been suggested.[12]

For the purposes of dating the Intermediate Orientalizing Complex at Poggio Civitate, it is possible to look to examples of such bucchero found in burials also containing a considerable quantity of narrowly datable Greek pottery. For example, Vetulonia's Tomba del Duce, excavated in the late nineteenth century, contained examples of both the Cerveteri and the northern types within one of its depositions.[13] In addition to this bucchero, the tomb also provided examples of Proto-Corinthian cups and skyphoi, a type of deep-bowled drinking vessel, dating from the second quarter of the seventh century BCE to the middle of the same century.[14]

The presence of numerous examples of both the Cerveteri and the northern types of this class of relief ware bucchero, coupled with a few sporadic fragments of Proto-Corinthian pottery recovered within the destruction debris of Poggio Civitate's Intermediate Orientalizing Complex, suggests that the construction of some or all of these buildings occurred within that time frame.

Alternatively, several scholars prefer a somewhat later date, looking to the technical sophistication of the various terracotta roofs associated with this phase of life at Poggio Civitate.[15] The techniques used to build these roofs, as well as thematic similarities to the iconography of Corinthian roofs assumed to be from the mid-600s BCE, contribute to arguments placing the date of these Poggio Civitate structures in the years around 640 or 630 BCE. However, these studies were completed before the discovery and excavation of the EPOC4 structure, as well as the subsequent revelation of elements of flanged terracotta tiles recovered beneath EPOC4's floor. Precisely how this new evidence relates to broader theories concerning the development of such roofs in central Italy remains under consideration.

Therefore, opinions as to the date of the construction of this complex of buildings depend to some degree upon which body of evidence a given observer chooses to emphasize. Scholars focusing on the technical form of Poggio Civitate's roofs of this period tend to prefer a date toward the end of the third quarter of the seventh century BCE for their construction. However, a considerable quantity of the ceramics recovered from the floors of the structures in the complex can be dated to the years around 675–650 BCE. Of course, we need not assume that the production date of such ceramics is consistent with the construction of the buildings in which they were recovered. However, the newly revealed architecture at Poggio Civitate described above suggests that some earlier theories concerning the date of the development of this technology may require reconsideration. Until a more definitive body of evidence emerges, it is perhaps wise to emphasize accuracy over specificity and simply conclude that the buildings of Poggio Civitate's Intermediate Complex were likely constructed around the middle of the seventh century BCE.

The technological shift to such durable roofing materials would considerably attenuate the functional life span of these buildings. Just as we note the coalescence of iconography designed to emphasize familial identity and descent from divinity (described below), the houses on which this iconography is displayed become suitable for multiple generations of occupation by the same family. Thus, we see in this technology the instrument that allows the Etruscan house—and the Roman *domus*—to serve as a physical metaphor for the elite, generational family identity it contained.

The Decorative Program of the Orientalizing Complex

Not only are all three buildings in the Orientalizing Complex unusually large for their time of construction and use, but they share a sophisticated decorative program (figs. 3.6–3.7). The current state of evidence suggests that the three structures had similar, if not identical, roofs. OC2/Workshop has the best-preserved roof, which allows detailed consideration of both the technical form of these roofs and their iconographic message.

One fragment of what appears to be an element of a raking sima was recovered from the northern flank of Piano del Tesoro

3.6. Intermediate Phase sima

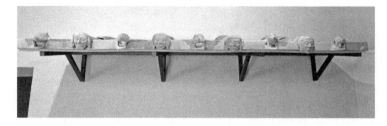

3.7. Intermediate Phase roof akroteria

3.8. Intermediate Phase raking sima fragment

(fig. 3.8).[16] This specimen, unique at Poggio Civitate, consists of the curved portion of the crowning element of the sima with an interior surface decorated by incised and painted tongue patterns. It is unlikely that all of the buildings of Poggio Civitate's Intermediate Phase employed such raking simae, but this fragment indicates that at least one, probably OC1/Residence, did.[17]

The lateral sima of the structures consisted of a pantile terminating in a low wall to catch rainwater, which was channeled down the roof. This water was directed through a perforation in the wall that was decorated on the exterior with a waterspout in the form of a feline (fig. 3.9). The outer edges of the sima wall were notched to receive a terminal cover tile, and each of these was capped with an antefix in the form of a female face (fig. 3.10).[18] Male antefixes displaying a short beard have also been recovered, although in considerably smaller numbers (fig. 3.11).[19] The mold for the production of this male antefix was recovered from the floor of OC2/Workshop, perhaps indicating that it was a later addition to the various buildings and their decorative programs.

The overall visual effect of the lateral sima's arrangement of repeating female faces and feline heads would have communicated a specific iconography: that of the Lady of the Animals.[20] This type

3.9. Intermediate Phase
feline waterspout

of iconography—representing a goddess connected to sex and fertility—was initially introduced into central Italy in the mid to late
eighth century BCE, and rapidly became among the most popular
types of representations of divinities in the decades that followed.[21]
While we do not know what she was named at Poggio Civitate, a
divinity associated with this iconography at a somewhat later period of Etruscan social development is called Uni, the Etruscan
counterpart to the Roman Juno.

The representation of this divinity is often found on material
included in elite graves of the seventh century BCE. In all likelihood, its inclusion in burial environments as well as on the roofs
of a series of monumental structures like those from Poggio Civitate is connected to the interest of Etruscan aristocrats in promoting themes connected to ancestry and progeny.[22]

At the top of the roof and attached directly onto the ridgepole
tiles was a series of akroteria.[23] Repeating images of stylized, triangular lotuses intertwined with palmettes of curving volutes

a

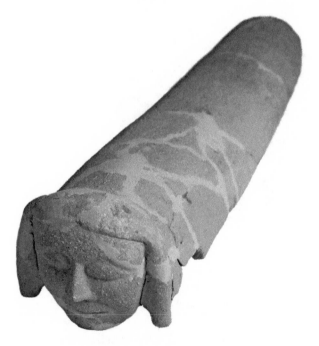

b

3.10. Intermediate Phase female antefix, shown (a) in front view and (b) capping roof tile

3.11. Intermediate Phase
male antefix

representing petals appeared on all three buildings (fig. 3.12). Some
examples of these lotus and palmette designs preserve indications
of red and white paint, although this additional decoration is not
well enough preserved on any example to allow us to determine its
original form. Other instances of similar designs show that incision
was sometimes used to accentuate designs.

Several additional types of figures were attached to the roofs of the other buildings. For example, an image of a horse and rider[24] (fig. 3.13) was recovered near the northern flank of OC1/Residence along with fragments of another animal figure, perhaps a feline of some form[25] (fig. 3.14). Smaller fragments of several different animal figures recovered from the destruction fills of these buildings suggest that all three roofs might have primarily displayed the lotus and palmette design, periodically punctuated with different types of figural images. Several, but not all, of these figural akroteria types also show that incision was employed to further clarify their designs. Some examples of akroteria fragments could be parts of either palmettes or the wings of fantastic creatures. For example, one such fragment[26] (fig. 3.15) preserves two curved but parallel incised lines connected by a series of diagonal, hatched lines, an effect that could have either complemented a floral design or represented the feathers of some form of winged creature.

At least one of the buildings also had a different type of crowning ornament at one of its ends. The findspot of this particular

3.12. Intermediate Phase lotus and palmette akroterion

3.13. Intermediate
Phase horse and rider
akroterion

3.14. Intermediate Phase
animal akroterion

akroterion[27] suggests that it was associated with OC1/Residence. Its decoration consists of two curving, volute-like projections that terminate in stylized feline heads (fig. 3.16). The felines bite into the body of the human figure located between them. It is unclear if a human head found near this element of sculpture was originally associated with it. It does not join to the feline faces and appears slightly larger in scale. If the head shown in figure 3.16 was not part of the original image, then the raised, circular area preserved

3.15. Intermediate Phase incised akroterion

3.16. Intermediate Phase human figure and felines akroterion

between the human figure's arms would presumably be the head, inverted and hanging from the animals' jaws.

Whether or not the larger head found nearby is original to the image, this male figure flanked by felines is likely a Master of Animals image, a male corollary to the female type with which it shares this iconography.[28] And yet, with this example and many others, the male figure is either bitten or consumed by the animal familiars. This apparently dichotomous feature of such images—the "master" overcome by the animals—is a type of figure consistent with an Etruscan understanding of the source narrative, in their version of which the male is often depicted being bitten or consumed by the animal familiars of the female divinity.[29]

That this image represents a Master of Animals is also implied by another element of these buildings' decorative program. Several examples of a bearded, male antefix type have been recovered from the destruction horizons of the three buildings. While not nearly as commonly represented as the female face type, this male antefix form was attached to the cover tiles in the same manner as the female antefixes described above (fig. 3.17). Therefore, when this antefix was in position, it would have been perceived as a male flanked by felines in a manner akin to that of the female faces.[30] The considerably smaller number of preserved examples of the bearded male, coupled with the fact that a matrix for the male's production was recovered from the floor of OC2/Workshop, may indicate that it was used as a replacement form when and where the original female types were damaged and required repair.

The incorporation of both Mistress and Master of Animals images into the decorative programs of the roofs of this complex suggests that the patrons and builders of the structures were familiar with the narrative sources of this iconography. The image of the female flanked by animals is among the oldest representations of a divinity. It is employed as early as the ninth millennium BCE in Jericho and gradually became a common means to both depict a goddess linked to sexuality and fertility and to describe a consortial relationship between the goddess and a mortal, male ruler or

3.17. Reconstruction of Intermediate Phase lateral sima

king. In its earliest surviving textual iterations, the female divinity is Ishtar. As the concept was carried westward, the name of the divinity changed while its iconographic expression remained recognizable. In the eastern Mediterranean, she was called Astarte, and in the Greek world, the concept was fractured into three distinct divinities—Artemis, Aphrodite, and Hera—all of whom were represented using aspects of the original iconography. When traders and merchants from the eastern Mediterranean brought knowledge of this divinity to the Etruscans, it was not limited to images of Astarte. This process of transmission must have also included some elements of the narratives associated with the divine characters.[31] Regardless of this possible iconographic interpretation, it is indisputable that these prominently displayed images would have been an impressive and ostentatious statement of the power and prestige of the individuals inhabiting the structures they adorned.[32]

Daily Life of the Social Elite of Poggio Civitate

The size of OC1/Residence stands in stark contrast to examples of domestic architecture located elsewhere on the hill and discussed below. With a total floor area of just under 300 square meters, OC1/Residence encompassed over fifteen times the living space of the houses belonging to the site's non-elite residents. The structure also provides an unusually clear view into the material world of members of the Etruscan aristocracy of this period. While some evidence suggests that materials of value were salvaged following the fire that destroyed all three buildings of the complex, considerable evidence of daily life was recovered during the excavation of OC1/Residence and environs.

Food storage and cooking appear to have largely taken place in

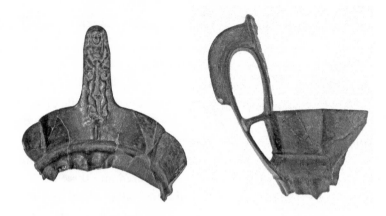

3.18. Bucchero cup from OC1/Residence

the northern end of the building. Several large dolii, some containing carbonized indications of grain, were countersunk beneath the
level of the building's floor.[33] Nearby were numerous examples of
cooking vessels, small braziers, and other forms of crockery needed
for food production and preparation.

Banqueting and tableware recovered within OC1/Residence
reflect a range of sources for luxurious, sometimes imported vessels. Ionian, Rhodian, Chiot, and Corinthian drinking vessels were
all recovered in high concentrations from the area of the building's northern extent.[34] Additionally, an exceptional bucchero banquet service also came from within this area, suggesting that the
members of this household regularly dined with distinctive, high-
quality ceramics (fig. 3.18).[35]

Furniture within the building was likely highly refined and elab-
orately decorated. The thousands of examples of bone and antler
inlay recovered from OC1/Residence's floor would have served to
ornament a number of wooden surfaces. Most are simple geomet-
ric designs consisting of triangles or meander patterns. Petal forms
appear quite frequently and likely were grouped into floral or rosette motifs. Several examples of figurines were also found. Some

display dowel holes on their undersides, indicating they were attached to larger objects such as boxes or pyxides[36] (fig. 3.19).

These charming and expertly carved bone, antler, and ivory figurines are worthy of appreciation in their own right. However, a group of similar carved plaques hint at ritualized behaviors and perhaps were even imagined to possess magical properties. One preserves the lower portion of a female figure wearing a gown[37] (fig. 3.20). An associated non-joining fragment bears a portion

3.19. Ivory or bone sphinx with dowel holes

3.20. Plaque depicting a gowned woman, obverse and reverse

of the figure's braids and arm, indicating that the original image showed this figure grasping her braids in a gesture consistent with numerous representations of the fertility goddess. However, the plaque did not serve as an inlay. This is shown by the presence of an inscription on its reverse displaying a woman's name, *ạσ vheiσalnạ*, transliterated as Vheisalna.[38]

Another example of such a plaque is still more curious.[39] This specimen is too fragmentary to allow identification of the representation on its obverse, although the preserved portions of its surface are suggestive of hair and a human shoulder (fig. 3.21). However, the inscription on its reverse consists of five letters preserving the name *]larθi[/*. Unlike other examples of such inscribed objects, the letters incised onto the surface of this example are so small as to be nearly invisible to the naked eye without the benefit of magnification.[40]

While such inscribed plaques are exceptionally rare, scholarly comment on them has largely come to the consensus that they served as *tesserae hospitals*, tokens used to identify the holder within the larger social tradition of reciprocal hospitality among the social elite.[41] Such tokens of recognition would be presented in courtly environments as evidence of the bearer's identity, although precisely how or why this would serve as a personal guarantee is now unclear. It should also be noted that both male and female names are found on these examples of figurines and plaques. Why women would move between communities without the benefit of escorts— and how they could do so safely—is equally unclear.

Another possible interpretation of these inscribed plaques is that they served as fertility totems. When it is possible to reconstruct the iconography of the obverse of such plaques, they consistently represent either the Etruscan divinity responsible for fertility or her animal familiars. The extraordinarily small letters of the *larθi* example support this possibility. Given their size, perhaps the primary intention of the inscriber was not to display the name, but to link the named person to the concept represented on its reverse by placing the inscription on the object.[42]

Measurements*

DL 0: 2.457 mm
DL 1: 1.543 mm
DL 2: 2.486 mm
DL 3: 2.379 mm
DL 4: 1.274 mm
DL 5: 1.782 mm
DL 6: 1.139 mm
DL 7: 1.005 mm
DL 8: 1.310 mm
DL 9: 1.257 mm
DL 10: 1.246 mm

* DL refers to 'Drawn Line' and the number
refers to the order in which it was drawn
and measured.

3.21. Inscription on reverse of plaque, with indications of letter sizes

While bronze appears to have been largely salvaged from the building immediately following the fire, some elements of bronze banqueting equipment were recovered during excavation. A bronze figurine in the form of a wrestler, a fragment of another wrestler's leg, and an umpire holding a staff were found on the building's floor (fig. 3.22). These figurines, which are missing their feet, appear to have broken off from a larger object, likely an ornamental stand of some kind.[43] Moreover, two examples of bronze cauldrons were found on the building's floor. One of these cauldrons has been comprehensively conserved and preserves a number of indications that it was repaired in antiquity with various patches, likely reflecting the frequent use of these kinds of items[44] (fig. 3.23). Curiously, at the time of conservation, an iron adze head was recovered from the vessel's interior, although what relationship the adze may have had to the cauldron is unclear. This reminds us that while much of OC1/Residence's banquet service is similar to examples included in the graves of the social elite, people used this equipment on a regular basis. As such, it formed an essential instrument that the people of Poggio Civitate likely used and saw on a daily basis, reflecting the elevated social status of those who possessed it.

3.22. Bronze figurines from OC1/Residence

3.23. Bronze cauldron and iron adze from OC1/Residence

Domestic industry is also reflected in a number of spindle whorls, rocchetti, and loom weights, which all suggest that fiber processing and textile production were features of daily life in OC1/Residence. However, it is interesting to note that spindle whorls of particularly small size and low weight are heavily concentrated within the building. While larger spindle whorls are also present within OC1/Residence, this cluster of smaller, lighter whorls speaks to an aspect of household production within this space. These lightweight spindle whorls are suited for the production of finer threads. Given this, the statistically significant number of smaller spindle whorls within OC1/Residence likely means that spinning within the elite residence focused on finer, more delicate threads, which presumably were then transformed into more refined textiles, at least in comparison to the fabric produced by the mostly larger spindle whorls distributed in the area of OC2/Workshop.

Other types of materials reflect a number of features of daily life. Cosmetic items in the form of bronze implements and ivory spoons perhaps represent the equipment of a woman's toilette. Small quantities of gold and silver jewelry similarly reflect the high status of the people to whom these materials belonged.[45] Fibulae[46] of a wide range, primarily in bronze but also occasionally in iron, were present in considerable concentration as well.[47] All of these materials il-

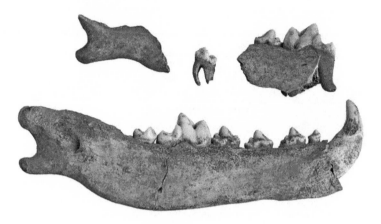

3.24. Fragments of wolf jaw from OC1/Residence

lustrate the varied and nuanced ways in which the building's residents used personal ornamentation and appearance as a means of ostentatious display.

Fishing, reflected by fishhooks present in OC1/Residence, appears to have been another activity engaged in by OC1/Residence's inhabitants.[48] Additionally, preserved portions of the skeletal remains of animals within OC1/Residence indicate that hunting was another preferred activity. Analysis of the bone assemblage within the building shows a disproportionate number of examples of the skeletal remains of red deer.[49] These animals were both non-domesticated and of considerable size. Additionally, wild pigs (locally known as *cinghiali*) of enormous size are also overrepresented in the OC1/Residence assemblage, as are examples of auroch and brown bears.[50]

One specific point of evidence related to hunting hints at some of the more complex ways in which trophies taken from slain animals can be used to describe power, privilege, and status.[51] One example preserves most of the lower jaw of a large wolf[52] (fig. 3.24). The left and the right sides of the animal's jaw were recovered in close proximity to each other. Since these portions of the skeleton are not fused, and no other portion of the animal's skeleton was recovered, it is likely that the jaw was originally attached to a pelt preserving the animal's head. It is possible that this wolf's pelt was present in the building as a trophy reflecting an elite male's dominion over a dangerous and hostile predator; alternatively, it may have been part of an ornamental, and possibly ceremonial, headdress of a kind seen elsewhere in Etruscan and Roman iconography.[53]

OC3/Tripartite and Connections to the Larger Etruscan World

Adjacent and perpendicular to OC1/Residence was the shorter, slightly wider structure now known as Orientalizing Complex Building 3/Tripartite (OC3/Tripartite). As mentioned above, this building's tripartite plan is suggestive of later examples of Etruscan religious architecture. The building lacks evidence of the podium or frontal colonnade characteristic of later temples, but was likely constructed prior to the codification of architectural formulae associated with such buildings.

Unfortunately, OC3/Tripartite was not as well preserved as either OC1/Residence or OC2/Workshop. The construction of the later Archaic Phase building appears to have damaged considerable portions of the earlier building's foundation walls. Moreover, some very early areas of excavation failed to recognize the structure's floor, resulting in some additional damage to its surface. As a result, when the building was re-examined from 1997 to 1999, only 9.5 square meters of the original 131.49 square meter interior floor area survived.[54] However, upon that area of the central cella's floor, excavation recovered several examples of unusual, non-local ceramics. While the overwhelming majority of ceramics recovered from the environs of both OC1/Residence and OC2/Workshop were locally manufactured, an unusually high percentage of the typologically identifiable ceramic specimens from OC3/Tripartite were manufactured in production centers such as Vulci, Cerveteri, and possibly Populonia or Vetulonia.[55]

In addition, excavation immediately south of OC3/Tripartite's southern foundation wall revealed traces of three circular cuttings

3.25. Circular cuttings into bedrock immediately south of OC3/Tripartite

into the underlying bedrock (fig. 3.25). While no obvious material explanation for these circular cuttings was found inside these holes, the sampled soil excavated from within them did contain an unusually high concentration of fatty alcohols. The meaning of this concentration of fatty alcohol was not immediately apparent, but it is noteworthy that both wax and animal fat were potential ancient sources of such long-chain alcohols.

The building's tripartite form and the unusual circular pits to its south both suggest that the structure served a religious function. Moreover, fragments of a stone altar, to be discussed below, were recovered from deposits associated with the site's ultimate, final destruction. These deposits were immediately south of OC3/Tripartite, perhaps indicating the altar's original position and pointing to a generations-long tradition of religious behaviors centered in this area. Moreover, several examples of non-local ceramics recovered from the floor in the middle of the central cella of OC3/Tripartite suggest another possible feature of religious behavior. These ceramics point to ritualized behaviors that connected Poggio Civitate's elite family to other aristocratic family groups throughout the Etruscan world.

Recovered from the middle of the central room's floor were fragments of conical base of an elegant type of bucchero kyathos (fig. 3.26).[56] This form of base is usually associated with the type of relief-ware bucchero discussed above and found in a number of extraordinarily wealthy burials in Cerveteri as well as at several localities along the northern and western edges of the Colline Metallifere. An inscription, assembled from several associated fragments, in letterforms characteristic of alphabets employed in southern Etruria, runs in a spiral fashion about the base. It reads:

mix[ ]urpaiθinaie[ ]ḷụ[ ]cẉ

The text conforms to known conventions associated with what are referred to as *muluvanike* inscriptions,[57] and can be reconstructed in its near-entirety to read: *miṇ[i velθ]ụr paiθinaie[mu]ḷụ[vani]cẉ*. This phrase is translated as "I am given by Velthur Paithinaie."[58]

Not only do several other examples of such relief-ware kyathoi preserve similarly placed inscriptions, but a few of those are identi-

3.26. Caeretan inscribed kyathos from OC3/ Tripartite

3.27. Northern type of inscribed vessel from OC3/Tripartite

fied by those inscriptions as originating from members of the same *paiθinaie* family.[59]

A second fragment of an inscribed kyathos was recovered only a few centimeters from the one described above (fig. 3.27). This example is also a fragment of a base.[60] Deeply incised interlocking lotus and palmettes run around the lower portion of the base, and portions of three letters survive above the lotus and palmette chain. While similar to the larger specimen, this example has a smaller diameter, and the incision work is notably less precise. However, the text represented by the three preserved letters can be partially reconstructed to read:

[mulu]vaṇ[ice]

This can be translated as: "XXX presented me as a gift."[61]

While these two cups with their inscriptions of donation were found close together on OC3/Tripartite's floor, their typological distinctions, differences in the firing process used to create the cups, and the epigraphic variations in the letterforms of the inscriptions on the cups all suggest that they originated from two different production centers.[62] However, it is striking that the same *gens*, or familial name, *Paithnas*, is associated with the individuals donating cups manufactured at two different production centers.[63]

The distribution of both versions of these vessels may hold a clue explaining why the *Paithnas* family was manufacturing and giving away cups of this type during the second quarter of the seventh century BCE. Cups of both the Cerveteri class and the northern class are found in burials from Cerveteri, but all other examples are found in either burials or habitation sites along the northern and western sides of the Colline Metallifere, with the single exception of Chiusi, slightly further to the west. If members of a community such as Cerveteri were interested in establishing relationships with communities throughout the Colline Metallifere, these drinking cups could have served to totemize such overtures. The considerable metal resources throughout the region encircled by the distribution of the cups would certainly be motivation for communities like Cerveteri to participate in a broader Mediterranean economy. For members of Poggio Civitate's social elite, the investiture of such vessels within a possibly religious building like OC3/Tripartite may have lent a degree of religious validation to the social and political relationships expressed by them.[64]

The possibility of a second, similar network of material exchange may be indicated by examples of another type of inscribed vessel also recovered at Poggio Civitate. These examples are both fragments of bucchero vessels preserving elements of similar *muluvanike* inscriptions.[65] However, the typological form of these vessels appears to be that of a specific type of bowl with projecting, terminal handles. Such "wing handle" vessels are well documented at Poggio Civitate as well as at a number of other communities throughout the inland area of central Italy.[66] However, the existence of a specific type of such vessel—with distinctive reticulated handles in the form of lotus palmettes, some of which preserve elements of *muluvanike* inscriptions—suggests that other families were engaging in a similar exchange of drinking cups. Preserved examples of such cups with inscriptions indicate that the family groups or individuals associated with this class of vessel were *keivale* and *aranθur*.

Cerveteri is also implicated in this network, as two examples of this type of vessel were recovered from that community.[67] However, the typological form of such "wing handle" vessels is generally characteristic of pottery production among communities of the central, inland areas of Etruria, suggesting that whomever *keivale* and *aranθur* represent, they were engaged in a similar form of gift exchange between communities to the north and west of Poggio Civitate.

In spite of the limited evidence for ritual behavior at Poggio Civitate, we can be confident that religious ideation infused any number of daily or periodic events. OC3/Tripartite's considerable size and the commonality of its decorative programs with those of OC1/Residence and OC2/Workshop further suggest that some form of religious behavior was supervised by Poggio Civitate's elite family, very likely for both social and political purposes.[68]

Manufacturing at Poggio Civitate

The state of preservation of OC2/Workshop is unique among known production centers of this period in central Italy. Materials recovered from the building's floor permit a detailed and nuanced consideration of a great number of different forms of production and manufacturing. Moreover, the distribution of materials across OC2/Workshop's floor also indicates that different areas of the building—at least at the time of its destruction—focused on different types of production.

Material associated with metalworking was recovered in high concentrations in the eastern extent of OC2/Workshop. For instance, resting directly on the building's floor were examples of equipment associated with a small foundry.[69] One feature of this foundry was a curious, multipart piece of equipment consisting of a ceramic object approximately in the shape of an isosceles triangle.[70] Two large, tubular perforations on the narrow end of the object meet within it and emerge from the opposite apex in a single hole (fig. 3.28). There is a small amount of vitrification visible on the apex end of the object, suggesting this portion of it was subjected to intense heat. In addition to this triangular object, several

3.28. Terracotta bellows nozzle from OC2/Workshop

3.29. Terracotta pipe with vitrification from OC2/Workshop

fragments of ceramic tubes or piping were also recovered (fig. 3.29), along with hundreds of fragments of crucibles and small ovens.

The ceramic tubing and triangular ceramic object are recognizable as portions of a double-action bellows. Bellows bags would force air from the dual perforations on the triangular object's base through its apex; these bags may have been made from the skin of an animal. The ceramic piping fit into the aperture of one of the small ovens, producing the evidence of intense burning localized around its narrowing nozzle.[71] Experimental metallurgy using modern copies of this equipment successfully melted copper and bronze ingots, demonstrating the likely ancient purpose of these materials.[72]

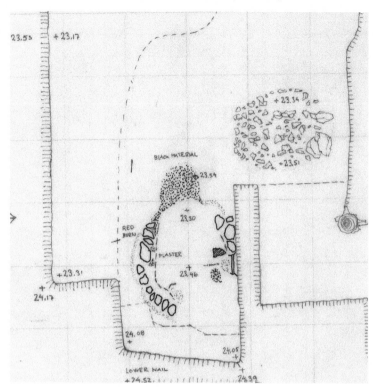

3.30. Plan of area around metal ore roasting oven

The heating of ores to extract metals took place at Poggio Civitate, but this activity was undertaken several hundred meters removed from Piano del Tesoro.[73] Two examples of simple, horseshoe-shaped stone constructions lined with plaster were located about 150 m northwest of OC2/Workshop. Heavy concentrations of ferric slag and burned material were seen at the apertures of these features, indicating their use for the roasting of copper ore (fig. 3.30).

Despite the immediate availability of copper ore from the hills adjacent to Poggio Civitate, the evidence of metal production does not suggest the large-scale conversion of ores into metals. Instead, the small scale of the preserved equipment indicates that metal production and the manufacture of small bronzes were probably episodic endeavors driven by immediate needs. Simple fibulae, nails and tacks, quotidian objects such as cosmetic implements, arrow points, and fishhooks would all easily have been produced within this area (fig. 3.31). Larger-scale bronze production at Poggio Civitate seems unlikely on present evidence, but it must be allowed that the intrinsic value and recyclable nature of bronze could obscure some evidence of this industry.

Another local resource that was exploited at considerable scale was clay. There is abundant evidence of pottery production and terracotta manufacturing within OC2/Workshop. Shortly before the building burned down, laborers formed a series of cover tiles and placed them in rows to dry in the shade of the roof. As the fire consumed the building, workers fled the space and stepped on the

3.31. Metal production equipment and small bronzes from OC2/Workshop

still-moist clay. The subsequent heat of the fire partially baked the tiles, leaving the impressions of the panicked workers' footprints (fig. 3.32).[74]

This interrupted effort to produce cover tiles was not the only aspect of terracotta and ceramic production underway at the time of the fire. Several examples of formed ribbons of clay had been placed on OC2/Workshop's floor several meters to the west of the cluster of unfired cover tiles.[75] While the intended purpose of these clay ribbons is not known, it is notable that they precisely match the dimensions of the frieze plaques associated with Poggio Civitate's Archaic Phase building, described below (fig. 3.33). If these were intended to serve as similar plaques, they would likely have been painted when complete. One fragment of such a painted plaque was recovered from Piano del Tesoro's northern flank, and could thus potentially be associated with OC1/Residence. This fragment confirms that such painted revetment plaques were known at the site during the intermediate phase of the community's monumental architectural development.[76]

Other forms of decorative architectural elements were also manufactured in OC2/Workshop. For instance, the mold for the production of the male antefix type described above was recovered resting on the building's floor (fig. 3.34).[77] While fewer examples of

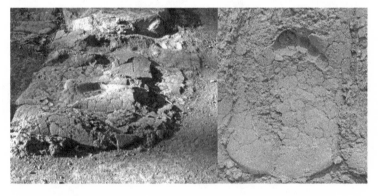

3.32. Unfired roofing tiles with human footprints from OC2/Workshop

3.33. Unfired possible revetment plaque from OC2/Workshop

this antefix type are preserved, its distribution across the plateau suggests that it was employed on some of the buildings of the complex. If so, the mold's presence in the building may indicate it was kept for the purpose of repairing or replacing antefixes as needed.

Other, more intimate expressions of clay-working are found throughout the area of OC2/Workshop. The fire that destroyed the building also baked a number of unformed, amorphous elements of clay that were found in highest concentration around the building's eastern extent. Several show clear indications of finger and palm impressions. One example[78] bears the indentation of a thumb and two fingers made as a small hand pulled wet clay from a source that likely rested on the building's floor. Another preserves the impression of a laborer's palm- and fingerprints; this person was clearly in the process of kneading the clay prior to positioning it on a wheel to transform it into a vessel (fig. 3.35).[79]

This same area of the building's western extent also preserves high concentrations of animal bone (fig. 3.36). Cut marks and indications of chopping are visible on hundreds of such bone fragments, indicating that the slaughter and butchering of animals was another feature of the building's production capacity.[80] The evidence of this process reflects some specific, reconstructible practices. For instance, virtually every example of the vertebrae of

3.34. Mold for human antefix from OC2/Workshop

sheep, goats, pigs, and cattle recovered within and around OC2/
Workshop is split through the approximate center of the spine. Observation of traditional butchering practices in the region around
Poggio Civitate today shows that a slaughtered animal is hung by
its hind legs and split down its center into two roughly equal halves
through the use of a hatchet or similar instrument.

3.35. Balls of clay with impressions of handprints from OC2/Workshop

3.36. Bone with indications of butchering from OC2/Workshop

The bone assemblage from OC2/Workshop indicates considerable exploitation of expected animal types. Pigs are well represented, constituting 50 percent of the total assemblage. Sheep and/or goats are the next most frequently slaughtered animal (25 percent of the total assemblage), while cattle are also present in slightly lower concentrations (20 percent of the assemblage). Other animals are present in lower quantities, including foxes and hares/rabbits, and five times more birds than other areas, all pointing to a broad exploitation of various species native to the area for food, bone, pelts, feathers, and other products such as milk, wool, and labor.

While "prestige hunting" animals are concentrated within the environs of OC1/Residence, the remains of one such animal—red deer—are present in high quantities within OC2/Workshop as well. These enormous creatures are not domesticated and the presence of their bones clearly reflects hunting activity. However, the red deer skeletal remains consist frequently of the bones of the animals' forelegs, which were typically cut bilaterally with the use of a rigid saw (fig. 3.37). Additionally, hundreds of examples of similarly cut elements of antler are found in comparable concentrations throughout OC2/Workshop.

The antler and bone elements were then further cut and polished into a range of small plaques and inlays. Guilloche (cable) patterns incised upon plaques approximately 1 cm in width are common, as are examples of plaques displaying simple meander patterns (fig. 3.38). Narrow half-round moldings are also common, as well as triangular plaques. Perhaps the most frequently preserved type of inlay have petal designs, and were presumably grouped together into rosette patterns or used in conjunction with triangular elements to form various motifs.[81]

Some partially completed examples of such objects reveal details of the technical process of production. For example, an extant portion of antler bears indications of several drill holes bored into one cleanly cut surface (fig. 3.39).[82] In fact, the gauge of the drill bit is even visible in several of the perforations. However, at the antler's

3.37. Partially worked and cut bone from OC2/Workshop

3.38. Bone plaque with incised guilloche pattern from OC2/Workshop

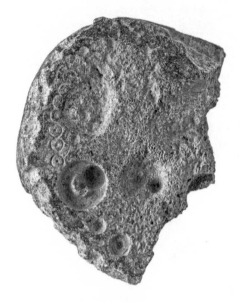

3.39. Antler with drill
holes

3.40. Fragment of ivory
writing tablet from
OC2/Workshop

edge, where the material is densest, an artisan carefully rendered
a partially complete guilloche pattern of a form notably similar
to that seen on several fragmentary examples of objects, such as a
writing tablet recovered adjacent to OC2/Workshop (fig. 3.40).[83]

A few examples of three-dimensional figurines or high-relief plaques were also recovered within OC2/Workshop's environs. One, a rather inelegantly rendered sphinx in antler, appears to have broken before it was completed, and was thrown into a midden located immediately north of the building's eastern extent (fig. 3.41).[84] Another example, this one a relief representation of a male profile also recovered from the same midden,[85] preserves indications of a guilloche pattern rendered on its reverse side, suggesting the object was being reworked from one form into another when it was discarded (fig. 3.42).

3.41. Antler sphinx figurine from OC2/Workshop

3.42. Plaque with human face from OC2/Workshop, obverse and reverse

3.43. Carved ivory or
bone human head from
OC2/Workshop

The range in the types of examples of worked bone, antler, and
ivory is considerable. For instance, PC 20070199 is an example of
carved bone or ivory, rendered in high relief (fig. 3.43).[86] The upper
surface of the face's head is flat, suggesting that details such as hair
or a headdress would have been added in another material. Moreover, the small, tabular projection below the face's chin suggests it
was slotted into another medium, perhaps wood, representing the
upper torso of the figure.[87]

Another common activity situated within OC2/Workshop involved the conversion of fibers into thread, yarn, and textiles
(fig. 3.44). Hundreds of examples of spindle whorls, concentrated
in the area north of the building, indicate that spinning was likely a
constant activity for some of the community's inhabitants.[88] These
spindle whorls are usually truncated, biconical forms, perforated
by a single, centrally located hole meant to receive a wooden spin-

dle stick. Whether these whorls served on the top or the bottom of weighted spindles cannot be determined. Many are decorated with dimples placed around the base of the cone, while others are ornamented with incised or stamped designs. However, one feature of many such spindle whorls that is often thought to be decorative in fact likely aids the process of thread production. Numerous whorls display fluting along the underside and sides of the whorl. Modern examples of spindle whorls show that these likely held thread in place during the spinning process. Thus, while aesthetically pleasing, these fluted whorls also helped anchor thread, making the spinning process more efficient.

Hundreds of examples of ceramic objects called rocchetti share a similar form but manifest a considerable range of sizes. Each is

3.44. Spindle whorls, rocchetti, and loom weights from OC2/Workshop

roughly tubular and terminates in flared, often domed, heads on either end that are usually about twice the diameter of the shaft. While many examples of rocchetti are decorated with incision or stamped motifs, these additions to the objects are exclusively found on the surface of the rocchetto's head.

The function of such rocchetti has been an issue of some discussion for several years. They are frequently regarded as spools for thread, but many modern weaving experts note that their size would make their service in this capacity rather inefficient. Instead, scholars versed in textile production largely interpret these types of objects as bobbins or small weights primarily associated with a type of textile production called tablet weaving. Tablet weaving, a process whereby flexible, perforated cards are strung into a small loom-like assembly, is used to make decorative ribbons of a type frequently represented throughout Etruscan tomb painting. This type of ribbon may also be displayed on the hem of a garment depicted on one of Poggio Civitate's seated akroteria associated with the site's Archaic Phase and discussed later in this book. In fact, visual analysis of a portion of preserved textile from one of Poggio Aguzzo's burials confirms that it was produced in this manner, demonstrating that the spinners and weavers of Poggio Civitate were familiar with this technological tradition.[89]

Personalities of Poggio Civitate's Workforce

The remarkably vivid material description of labor and manufacturing preserved within the environs of OC2/Workshop is well documented. The panicked flight from the building preserved by the workers' footprints in the wet clay of unfinished roof tiles captures a moment in time.[90] Small, humble objects such as the elements of unworked clay preserving finger- and palm prints do the same, allowing modern observers to place their hands into the voids left by these remote and anonymous individuals who lived and labored within this space.

Several objects recovered within the area of OC2/Workshop

3.45. Inscribed rocchetto from OC2/Workshop

provide other glimpses into facets of the identity and circumstances of these people. One is a fragment of an impasto rocchetto (fig. 3.45).[91] Carefully incised onto its shaft are four letters forming the word *RIXA*.[92] This word is not attested elsewhere in the Etruscan language, so there can be no confidence in its translation into modern English. Puzzlingly, if thread were wound around its shaft, either as a spool or as a bobbin, the word would be obscured. *RIXA* could refer to the object or potentially the object's use. However, the morphology of the word closely corresponds to our linguistic expectation of a feminine personal name.[93]

If so, who was *RIXA*? Why would her name be inscribed on the shaft of a rocchetto, indeed the only known example of an inscribed rocchetto anywhere in the region? Do we imagine *RIXA* was sufficiently literate to place her own name on this object? Clearly, certainty is impossible on such a point, but given what we know of literacy in early Etruria, it is extraordinarily difficult to imagine that someone of such simple estate as a woman engaged in labor within a space like OC2/Workshop would enjoy the advantages of literacy.[94] Was *RIXA* a young woman whose beauty caught the eye of

3.46. Possible "Turkish" spindle whorl element

a literate craftsperson also present within the building? We cannot know, but such glimmers of evidence invite passing speculation.

Another everyday object hints that someone else who was active within the area of OC2/Workshop may have experienced quite a different life story.[95] This puzzling object is an intact oblong piece made of carved horn, evenly tapering at both ends with a slight curve in its center (fig. 3.46). The middle of the object is transversely perforated by a single bore hole. However, the perforation is not circular as if created by a drill, like the perforation on the antler element described above. Instead, the sides of the perforation are squared. Moreover, visual analysis shows that the interior faces of the perforation are similarly squared, suggesting that an oblong object with a squared section was to be inserted into the hole.

The function of this unusual specimen of worked antler is not readily obvious. It could have served as a cleat or fastener, although the single perforation would not be suitable for securing it without its spinning or rotating. While the squared interior of the perforation could have helped prevent such slipping, the form of the object is notably suggestive of a specific type of spindle whorl, the "Turkish" spindle whorl (fig. 3.47), which consists of three separate elements: two interlocking crosspieces held in place by the spindle stick. The traditional moniker "Turkish" is a misnomer. Instead, this style of spindle whorl is characteristic of the Indo-Iranian plateau. Unfortunately, no comprehensive study of this type of spindle whorl has determined its chronological or geographical range. Since most examples are made from wood, there is little chance of the elements of such a spindle whorl surviving from antiquity unless recovered from unusual circumstances.

If this example of carved horn is a portion of such a spindle whorl, it is the only known example of one at Poggio Civitate or anywhere else in the region. This fact requires caution in coming to such a conclusion. However, if the element of horn is a portion of a modular type of instrument associated with thread production, it reflects a completely different technological sensibility than the hundreds of conical spindle whorls from Poggio Civitate and tens of thousands known from the region beyond the site. If it is a type of spindle whorl native to the Indo-Iranian plateau, its existence at Poggio Civitate likely reflects the presence here of someone from that area. Of course, the widespread association between spinning and textile production and the sphere of women invites us to imagine that the person who created this style of spindle whorl was a woman, perhaps an enslaved girl brought to Poggio Civitate who fashioned a spindle that reminded her of home.[96]

At least one inscription, recovered from a deposit a few meters west of OC2/Workshop and incised onto local ceramic, was composed using an Umbrian rather than an Etruscan alphabet (fig. 3.48).[97] The word preserved on the ceramic appears to be the name of an individual to whom or for whom the vessel (or its contents) was created. The name itself also appears to be Umbrian rather than Etruscan in derivation.[98] However, the elemental signa-

3.47. Modern example of a "Turkish" spindle whorl

3.48. Vessel fragment with Umbrian inscription

ture of the ceramic of the vessel is consistent with that of other examples of pottery produced at Poggio Civitate, pointing to a nominally polyglot community within OC2/Workshop's production
space.

While these three examples of materials cannot definitively link
us to the circumstances of the lives of workers engaged in OC2/
Workshop, they do offer a suggestion of a socially complex, ethni-
cally and linguistically diverse group active at the site. Whether
these people were chattel slaves or valued contributors to the industrial capacity of the site, lived experiences like theirs are only
rarely preserved in the archaeological record. The chance that Poggio Civitate might preserve echoes of these experiences reminds
us that populations and people of communities both ancient and
modern are constantly in flux, evolving and changing in response
to people and influential personalities often lost to history.

The Economy of Poggio Civitate

Several aspects of the labor housed in OC2/Workshop were focused on the concerns of the site's elite population. While roofing tiles are usually not thought of as related to high-status manufacturing, the building that was clearly in its planning stages—as reflected by the roofing tiles, revetment plaques, and ornamental antefixes produced in OC2/Workshop—suggests an ornamented structure communicating predictable themes of elite identity and iconography.

Considerable time and labor would have been required to ornament the wooden surfaces of furniture with the types of inlay found in such abundance within the building's environs. This too suggests that another feature of activity and industry housed in OC2/Workshop was directed toward elite consumption.

The intrinsic value of metals such as the bronze worked around OC2/Workshop's eastern extent are also plausibly linked to such concerns. The full extent of the community's bronzeworking industry is difficult to assess, given the recyclability of the metal, but the labor and resources required to extract copper and tin from available local deposits would have been considerable.

Several aspects of the food production visible within OC2/Workshop also suggest a connection to the consumption habits of the community's elite family. The analysis of animal bones both from the area of OC2/Workshop and from OC1/Residence shows a clear statistical preference for the consumption of the right side of animals within OC1/Residence, particularly for the forelimb of pigs and sheep/goats. In total, 66 percent of the pig and sheep/goat ulnae (a bone of the elbow) from OC2/Workshop are derived from the slaughtered animal's left side, while virtually the same percentage of ulnae collected from OC1/Residence for those two species are from a given animal's right side.[99] We cannot say why the residents of OC1/Residence preferred meat from an animal's right side, but the fact that they did, coupled with the statistically significant preference for animals' left sides in the environs of OC2/

Workshop, again suggests some form of specified connection between the activities and production housed in OC2/Workshop and the community's ruling family.

Given the obvious scale of the site's production capacity, it is curious that virtually nothing manufactured in the environs of OC2/Workshop has been found at sites beyond Poggio Civitate. While future discoveries could change this situation, only a few examples of carved bone plaques, recovered from elite burials at Castellina in Chianti and at Quinto Fiorentino, appear to be examples of the efforts of workers from Poggio Civitate.[100] Other forms of bone and antler products, Poggio Civitate's typologically distinctive ceramics, and the other materials clearly produced within OC2/Workshop are found only at Poggio Civitate itself. In spite of the enormity of the production space, the current state of evidence indicates that Poggio Civitate did not engage in meaningful export of the items manufactured there.

So why build and maintain a monumental, highly ornamental industrial center? One explanation is that Poggio Civitate's economy, at least as it is reflected in OC2/Workshop and other features of the site's production capacity, was inwardly directed. Raw materials, harvested agricultural produce, and animals for slaughter would be brought to OC2/Workshop, where these materials would be converted into useable commodities. Absent evidence for the broader export of those finished materials, we must assume these goods were locally consumed. One reasonable explanation is that OC2/Workshop served as a visual, physical expression of economic relationships between Poggio Civitate's leadership and the immediately surrounding, non-elite community. The building's decoration, an iconographic statement of the ruling family's descent from divinity, stood above a space wherein individuals produced luxury objects, some or most of which were consumed by that same elite family. The non-elite community's subordinate role in this production system was at least in part the result of the success of the propaganda expressed by the complex's decorative program.[101] Conceivably, some degree of redistribution of goods and services controlled by the patrons of OC2/Workshop helped to further facilitate a system designed primarily to benefit the ruling elite.[102] However, the products consumed by the site's aristocracy were likely designed and selected to further reinforce this disparity of material opportunity within the broader community.

Sigla and the Communitarian Environment of Poggio Civitate

One potential manner in which these sorts of social and economic arrangements were expressed may be seen in the corpus of *sigla*[103] preserved on a small percentage of roofing tiles and ceramics. The markings were placed on both pantiles and cover tiles while the clay was still moist prior to firing (fig. 3.49). In most circumstances, it appears that a finger was used to make these symbols, although a few examples appear to have been marked by a narrow stick or stylus. Examples of *sigla* on pottery are about equally divided between those placed on the vessel before it entered the kiln and those incised onto the surface after the firing process (fig. 3.50).

3.49. Pantile marked with *siglum*

3.50. *Siglum* on base of vessel

In total, twenty-two different *sigla* are found on the roofing tiles from Poggio Civitate. Of this number, eight or possibly nine are letters and thirteen are non-alphabetic symbols.[104] Similar symbols are found on examples of roofing tiles and ceramics from a number of other sites throughout the region.[105] However, at Poggio Civitate, the clearer view of the buildings' forms and functions, coupled with evidence of the broader community, permits some speculation as to their purpose at the site.

At Poggio Civitate, *sigla* placed on roofing elements are found only on cover tiles and pantiles. These types of tiles could be placed anywhere on a roof, apart from a few prescribed positions that required differently shaped pieces. These include raking sima elements that would have had to be placed on the diagonal eve of a building, lateral sima elements that could only be placed along a given structure's lateral sides, and ridgepole tiles, which necessarily must have been placed at a roof's apex. Curiously, only pantiles and cover tiles bear *sigla*. Raking sima, lateral sima, and ridgepole tiles never display such markings. Therefore, it seems unlikely that the markings somehow relate to a given tile's intended position on the roof of the building.

When the size of Poggio Civitate's various buildings is considered, another possible explanation for the *sigla* placed on roof tiles emerges, suggesting that these markings were associated with different, discrete groups of laborers. Given the known length of each building and the standard width of pantiles employed at the site, it is possible to make some informed estimates as to the total number of such tiles required to cover a particular building. For example, the preserved length of OC1/Residence is approximately 36.8 m. Since the standard width of pantiles used at the site is 0.54 m (as discussed above in relation to EPOC4), a total of sixty-eight such tiles would have been needed to cover a single register of the building's roof. Although pantiles vary to some degree, they are about 0.80 m in length. These dimensions would require that approximately eight registers of pantiles be laid out to cover the expanse of OC1/Residence's roof. Therefore, it is reasonable to assume that approximately 544 pantiles were employed to cover the building.

Each pantile weighs approximately 22 kg, meaning that the total weight of those tiles can be estimated to have been around 12,000 kg in total.[106] Employing the same logic, the number of tiles needed to roof the other buildings of the complex are:

OC2/Workshop: 54 m total length = 100 tiles per register. The building's width assumes 10 registers. Therefore, approximately

1,000 pantiles in total were required to roof OC2/Workshop, at an estimated weight of about 22,000 kg.

OC3/Tripartite: 24.4 m total length = 45 tiles per register. The building's width assumes 8 registers. Therefore, 360 pantiles were required to roof OC3/Tripartite, at an estimated weight of 7,920 kg.

Adding to this are the cover tiles that lay over the space between parallel sides of the pantiles. These would have totaled approximately 1,900 in number and weigh about 8 kg per unit, meaning that the total weight of clay needed for the cover tiles of these roofs would have been just over 15,000 kg.[107]

Therefore, it is reasonable to estimate that approximately 57,000 kg[108] of fired terracotta in the form of pantiles and cover tiles were incorporated into the roofs of the three buildings of Poggio Civitate's Intermediate Complex. Obviously, the raking and lateral simae, as well as the ridgepole tiles and their attached akroteria, would have added still more weight.

Given these specifications, we might ask the obvious question: who provided the labor and materials needed to excavate the clay from local sources, clean and levigate that clay, form it in molds, and gather the fuel required to operate the kilns in which they were fired? Clearly, a labor force of some size was present at Poggio Civitate, even if our evidence for their place in the community is limited. However, if Poggio Civitate's leaders were able to draw on the demographic resources of nearby communities, it is possible to imagine a large enough group of people to achieve such a task in a reasonable period of time.

One possible explanation for the placement of *sigla* on a small percentage of pantiles and cover tiles employed on buildings at Poggio Civitate is this: specific *sigla* were placed on representative examples of tiles produced by different groups of individuals charged with the production of materials required to realize large-scale building projects.[109] Larger groups or communities, such as one represented by the more common glyphs, like an *alpha* or an *X* sign, would presumably reflect the efforts of larger communities under the political control of Poggio Civitate's elite family. Smaller groups, such as those connected with glyphs such as the *rama secco* or a spiral design, would thus be asked to provide smaller contributions of materials to a collective effort. The teams of tile-makers associated with Poggio Civitate may have identified their labor in a manner similar to stone masons from an early date elsewhere in Italy.[110]

Non-Elite Domestic Spaces at Poggio Civitate

Some members of these subordinate populations lived in small spaces located to the south and west of Piano del Tesoro. Unfortunately, this area of Poggio Civitate has been subject to rather heavy erosion over the years. As a result, traces of these domiciles survive only in areas where outcroppings of bedrock served to naturally retain soil and hold in place those remains. Nevertheless, the surviving evidence permits a view into aspects of the material circumstances of these people.

At least two phases of simple domestic structures were first identified in 2012 and 2013 several meters to the southwest of Piano del Tesoro (fig. 3.51).[111] The best-preserved of these houses also appears to be the latest of the cluster of small houses, dating to the late seventh century BCE and thus contemporaneous with the later stages of the Intermediate Orientalizing Complex. However, the most obvious contrast between the buildings of the aristocratic complex and this structure is size. Although the northern portion of the building is lost to erosion, if we assume a structure roughly twice as long as its width, the interior floor space can be reconstructed to have been approximately 12 square meters. If so, the domestic space of the inhabitants of this structure was less than 1/12 that of the elite family occupying OC1/Residence.[112] Moreover, there is no clear evidence of terracotta roofing or the associated decorative features characteristic of the buildings of the Intermediate Complex to the north-

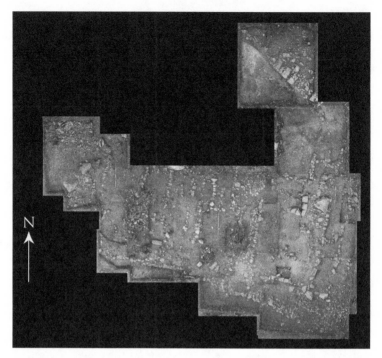

3.51. Aerial view of Civitate A non-elite domestic architecture

east. Therefore, this appears to be a comparatively modest dwelling and would have appeared especially so in comparison to the buildings of monumental scale with which they shared the hilltop.

However, a few items recovered from the structure suggest that its inhabitants enjoyed some degree of social standing within the community. Among these finds are the types of ceramics expected from a quotidian living environment, such as simple terracotta vessels, several of which preserved indications of burning on their interior surfaces suggesting they served as cooking instruments. Yet other examples imply a slightly greater degree of refinement, including fragments of ornamented pottery, including a vessel with a handle decorated with stamped designs of hatched triangles otherwise unparalleled at Poggio Civitate.[113] A fragment of a bucchero ribbon handle associated with a type of kyathos dating to the mid-seventh century BCE and displaying cylinder stamp decorations was also found within this space.[114] Perhaps notably, an example of a fragment of a similar vessel was also found within OC1/Residence. However, the overwhelming majority of ceramics recovered from within and around this space were simple, utilitarian styles of wares produced in local impasto and coarse wares. This evidence, alongside a number of examples of sheep, goat, pig, and cow bones bearing traces of cutting and chopping, points to everyday obligations of food preparation taking place within this structure.

As would be expected in a domestic space, evidence of fiber spinning and weaving was also present. Numerous simple spindle whorls and rocchetti were recovered, as well as a loom weight. However, while the total number of spindle whorls recovered (fifteen) is not large enough to permit broader statistical analysis, it may be revealing that no examples of the lighter, smaller spindle whorls found in abundance in OC1/Residence were recovered within this building. Therefore, it seems likely that textile production within this small household focused on weaving the coarser fabrics that would have resulted from the thicker yarns created by heavier spindle whorls.

Other aspects of household industry are reflected in the remains of bone, horn, and antler carving within the building. Dozens of examples of such materials preserve indications of cutting with the use of a rigid saw. One example is a portion of antler cut in the shape of a pyramid and attached to a circular element of the animal's skull (fig. 3.52).[115] The point of attachment to the skull is worked smooth and displays indications of numerous cut marks. The precise function of this object is not obvious, but it appears to have served as a working surface for small items. Several additional examples of small plaques, dowels, and beads were recovered and likely produced within this space.

Evidence of metalworking is concentrated outside of the structure and a few meters to the west.[116] Crucibles, vitrified terracotta surfaces preserving concentrations of slag, and numerous examples of ferric slag point to the extraction of copper from local ores. While

3.52. Worked horn possibly used as working surface

not great in number, a few interesting examples of bronze objects were recovered from the environs of the building. One, a fibula of the navicella variety, displays ornamental finials projecting from its arc (fig. 3.53).[117] This type of fibula is not unparalleled at Poggio Civitate but is among the rarer types found at the site. Additionally, excavation of this building produced a fragment of a bronze brooch or fastener of a type unique at Poggio Civitate but found elsewhere in mid-seventh-century Etruria. This two-pronged brooch would function in conjunction with another element that slotted into the squared holes on either prong and was fastened by means of a central hook and eye (fig. 3.54).[118] This type of fastener is quite rare and only otherwise paralleled in silver or gold forms from sites such as Cerveteri, Veii, Praeneste, and Casale Marittimo.

Another object recovered from the environs of this building is similarly curious. This specimen is a fragment of a small ceramic humanoid figurine (fig. 3.55).[119] The suggested form of a head and face was created by the simple process of pinching the sides of a ball-shaped element of clay, with the attached, narrower element below representing the neck. Nothing directly comparable to this object is found elsewhere at Poggio Civitate, but the form is strikingly similar to examples of stylized human figurines infrequently included in Latian burials, as well as humanoid figures, sometimes

3.53. Navicella fibula from non-elite household

3.54. Bronze two-pronged brooch from non-elite domestic context

applied to ceramics as decorative finials or handles, seen in the region near Chiusi, where they have been connected to possible traditions of ancestral veneration.[120] The function and purpose of this ceramic figurine fragment are unclear. However, it is inviting to speculate that the object was originally an example of a human figure, present in the household as a primordial expression of belief akin to that of the later tradition of the Roman *lares*. If so, the presence of this figure, along with the handful of more stylish items recovered from the floor, suggests that this household, while modest and humble, was likely not that of an enslaved individual or group. Instead, the occupants of this house appear to have been engaged in the exercise of daily life, cooking, and simple household industries, presumably for their own consumption and benefit. Moreover, they may have possessed a sufficient degree of social standing and familial identity to allow them to venerate a concept of their own ancestry, even if they did so with simple means in comparison to the ostentation and scale of the elite family residing only a few meters away.

The other examples of houses within this area—as well as a domestic space excavated several meters to the east in 2019—are not as well preserved. Nevertheless, materials recovered within their environs are similarly suggestive of a degree of domestic industrial autonomy. Evidence of small-scale metalworking, fiber-spinning equipment, and various forms of crockery all indicate that the inhabitants of these non-elite households were capable of subsistence-level household production and likely engaged in the daily struggle to collect and prepare food, to adequately clothe themselves, or to repair their basic thatched roofs when the need arose. In short, they lived simple lives within these spaces, but the aristocratic family of Poggio Civitate could call on their strength, energies, and abilities to produce materials as needed, or possibly ask them to defend the community from potential threats from beyond. It is possible to imagine that such services resulted in largesse from the community's leaders, taking the form of small trinkets of personal ornamentation or elegant ceramic vessels, reflective of aristocratic

3.55. Ceramic humanoid figurine fragment

luxury and likely starkly contrasting with the spare simplicity of the households on which they were bestowed.

Subordinate Communities beyond Poggio Civitate

The efforts of several teams of scholars working in the area around Poggio Civitate have shown that multiple communities were located along the chain of hills separating the Colline Metallifere and the Crete Senesi (fig. 3.56).[121] Of these communities, only that of Vescovado di Murlo has benefited from some degree of archaeological excavation.

Chamber tombs were discovered in 1960 in a section of Vescovado di Murlo called Tinoni during the construction of a building.[122] Materials ranging in date between the mid to late sixth century and the mid-third or second century BCE indicate that the population living in this area not only chronologically overlapped to some degree with the community of Poggio Civitate, but continued to exist even after Poggio Civitate's destruction and abandonment.

Another chance discovery of evidence of a community in Vescovado di Murlo occurred in 1970 with the construction of a road intended to bypass the central portion of the town to the west of Tinoni. This area, traditionally called Colombaio, was already known to Bianchi Bandinelli, who claimed to have been shown several examples of burials sporadically recovered in this area by local farmers.[123] The construction of the road, Via Martiri di Rigo Secco, cut through a portion of a large stone wall and revealed traces of two architecturally conjoined kilns. The wall runs parallel to the kilns' aperture along an east–west axis. One kiln space was squared and supported by a series of ceramic blocks. The second, southerly kiln was circular and partially destroyed by the road's construction.[124]

Reexamination of these kilns in 2006, in conjunction with additional excavation, revealed traces of domestic spaces south of the wall.[125] Simple ceramics, cooking wares, loom weights, and other features of daily life were all recovered from the floors of these

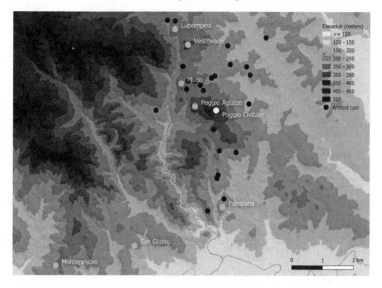

3.56. Distribution of regional settlements near Poggio Civitate

structures. Datable materials from this context suggest that these buildings were destroyed around the fourth century BCE. However, excavation beneath the floors produced fragments of ceramics both typologically and materially consistent with wares from Poggio Civitate from the sixth century BCE.[126]

Excavation in 2015, 2016, and 2017 in the area immediately west of these structures revealed a dramatic rise in elevation, leading to a higher terrace.[127] The terrace was bisected by a deep trench or moat, within which the wall first revealed in 1970 was shown to be set (fig. 3.57). This wall continued 14.30 m to the west before turning and ending in a finished face. Extraordinarily high concentrations of architectural debris, pottery, and animal and human bone were recovered inside the fill of the moat within which the wall was constructed. All of this material was chronologically consistent with the materials from the floors of the houses excavated in 2006. This indicates that a community at Vescovado di Murlo was contemporaneous with at least the final phase of Poggio Civitate's habitation, continued as a community for several centuries after Pog-

3.57. Portion of terrace wall in Vescovado di Murlo

gio Civitate's destruction, and suffered a serious reversal sometime in the late fourth or early third century BCE.

While not as clearly understood, other sites in the immediate area preserve traces of habitation also contemporary with Poggio Civitate's floruit. These include Pompana, Lupompesi, Murlo, and several others.[128] The presence of these communities offers a potential explanation as to how Poggio Civitate's leaders managed to design and execute structures of such considerable scale. Conceivably, upon deciding to embark on the ambitious building programs that would result in Poggio Civitate's various phases of monumental architecture, they may have asked or compelled members of these peripheral communities to supply specific quantities of the materials needed to build a given structure. This material and labor would include the collection of suitable stone for foundations—much of which would be readily available on Poggio Civitate itself—timber for a building's infrastructure, wattle and a sufficient quantity of daub for walls, and of course, roof tiles—the only element of this marshalling of resources that survives in any quantity.

Given this wider regional picture, is it not unreasonable to speculate that glyphs applied to roofing tiles before firing in a kiln were intended to track contributions of tiles associated with different groups of individuals or communities under the broader control of Poggio Civitate's leading family. If so, this would imply that a number of different groups were conscripted into a manufacturing process that symbolically represented the authority of multiple generations of the aristocratic family of Poggio Civitate through the monumentality of their domestic spaces.

It is possible to envision a similar explanation for *sigla* found on Poggio Civitate's ceramics. Precisely how Poggio Civitate's aristocrats exercised this degree of political control is unknown to us. However, features of religious behavior described below suggest that one social responsibility of the community's elite involved the performance of religious spectacles. It is not unreasonable to assume that the community engaged in predictable, seasonal festivals to mark the harvest or the return of spring, nor is it unlikely that other kinds of ad hoc or episodic events, such as births, marriages, or deaths, would also occasion religiously organized communitarian behaviors. One likely feature of such events would have been communal banqueting, for which these monumental buildings clearly possessed a capacity.

Indeed, evidence for communal banqueting is potentially reflected in a deposit of ceramics recovered several meters to the northeast of OC1/Residence. This deposit, from an area of excavation called Tesoro Trench 18, consisted of hundreds of examples of simple impasto and lower-quality bucchero versions of nearly identical shallow bowls resting on conical bases. These vessels, as well as the high quantity of refined local and imported ceramics recovered from OC1/Residence, represent a banquet service far greater in size than could possibly have been necessary for the inhabitants of OC1/Residence alone. Perhaps tellingly, a deposit of approximately one hundred identical shallow bowls set on conical bases was recovered from Tesoro Trench 18; five of these were marked with identical *sigla* (fig. 3.58). A letterform resembling *chi*

a

b

3.58. Example of vessel with *siglum* (a) and possible associated banquet service (b)

was placed on the attachment point between the base and bowl of these five vessels prior to firing, perhaps indicating that this collection of identical vessels was manufactured in a single batch.[129]

Conceivably, large-scale public events that involved communitarian banqueting, wherein different groups of people or different communities provided portions of the equipment and material for the celebration, could have required a tracking system similar to that envisioned for the roof tiles, described earlier. At times, or for certain types of events, these spikes in production would potentially have included pottery from different groups identified by specific *sigla*, resulting in the system of glyphs preserved on a small percentage of ceramics from the site.

Conviviality, Banqueting, and the Mistress of Animals

One specific kind of drinking vessel recovered in considerable numbers within OC1/Residence and its environs is a type of kyathos with ornamental handles. The form of the bowl varies, as does that of the base, but the common characteristics of this kind of kyathos are molded handles. While there is some variation among the types, the form of the handles resembles a female, often depicted with wings (fig. 3.59). In some instances, her hands angle across her torso, gripping braids hanging from her shoulders. In other versions, she grasps the paws of felines or is otherwise flanked by animals.[130] Again, this is the Mistress of Animals, a motif inextricably connected to concepts of fertility and procreation. Vessels with similar handles are known throughout the region from burials of approximately the same period, but the Poggio Civitate group appears to have been manufactured from local clay sources and displays several distinctive stylistic characteristics that indicate they were produced at the site.[131]

These drinking cups provide an opportunity to consider a feature of the visual environment of banqueting at Poggio Civitate. The inclusion of an image of a fertility divinity on a vessel associated with drinking is surely not arbitrary. In fact, evidence from

3.59. Drinking vessel
with ornamental handle

elsewhere in Italy points to a conceptual relationship between divinities associated with sexuality and the consumption of wine.[132]

The inclusion of images of the Etruscan version of a fertility goddess on vessels used for wine consumption in environments other
than funerary ones can be understood as communicating the same
theme. Moreover, we can imagine that within the visible, performative space of a public banquet at a place like Poggio Civitate,
such cups (and the distribution of their contents) would communicate a number of meaningful themes. Not only would the wine
drinkers themselves be connected to the idea of sex and fertility, but their surroundings—the iconographic and propagandis-
tic arguments presented on the exterior of the buildings around
them—could represent the claim that the site's leading family was
descended from an ancestor's sexual liaison with the goddess depicted on the wine cups. Conceivably, in a society where the ruling elite distributed certain elements of their material status back
to the broader community, one conceptual addition to that lar-

gesse may have been the idea that a blessing of fertility would be bestowed upon loyal lieutenants or trusted members of the subordinate groups around the architectural complex and wider area.

Responses to Death at Poggio Civitate

Poggio Aguzzo, the name associated with the extreme western extent of Poggio Civitate itself, served as a burial area for some members of the community. Sporadic recovery of objects from this part of the hill sparked any number of local legends about the chance discovery of warriors buried in golden armor. However, the archaeological reality of this burial area is somewhat more nuanced and considerably less romantic.

In 1972, limited excavation alongside a small farmhouse located atop this portion of Poggio Aguzzo resulted in the recovery of nine burials. Each consisted of a simple fossa, oriented on an approximately east–west axis. Soil conditions were such that most of the graves had failed to preserve skeletal material. However, in the few that did it appears that the heads were placed at one end of the grave, and offerings of ceramics were grouped at the feet of the individuals.[133]

Three burials included spears positioned on either side of the body. The presence of these objects might be suggestive of some aspect of the social identity or behavior of the individual buried, but the position of the spearheads and associated iron counterweights may also indicate that they served as the sides of a bier that carried the body from Poggio Civitate to Poggio Aguzzo. Knife blades were also included in two graves, while a small iron dagger in a wooden sheath was placed in a grave—Tomb 5—containing a notably higher-than-usual number of associated ceramics.

Several of the spearheads, spear counterweights, and knife blades from Tombs 1 and 5 preserve indications of mineralized textiles from garments or cloth originally included in the graves. For example, an iron knife blade recovered from Tomb 4 bears traces of a textile wrapped around both the flat surface and the edges,

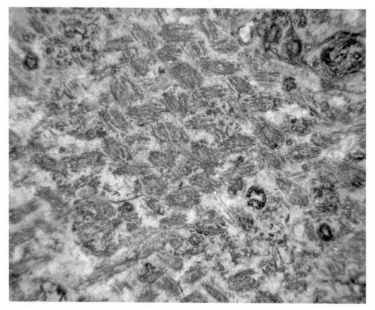

a

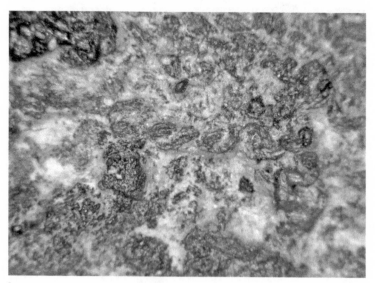

b

3.60. Preserved tabby weave textile (a) and preserved texile with decorative tassel (b)

3.61. Tablet weave impression from Poggio Aguzzo

indicating the cloth was originally wrapped entirely around the blade, perhaps as a sheath. In this instance, the textile was a simple tabby weave, although the vestiges of a tassel hint at a slightly more ornamented form (fig. 3.60).[134]

A different type of textile pattern, a twill weave, is preserved on elements of another textile from a Tomb 1 counterweight. The second counterweight from this burial also preserves traces of textile, although in this instance the preserved pattern is indicative of a tablet weave. The tablet weave, which would have formed a decorative border of some kind, was produced with at least seventeen tablets alternating 3Z3S threads (fig. 3.61). In all cases where indications of textiles are preserved on metal objects from these Poggio Aguzzo tombs, the fibers employed were wool.

Most of the pottery placed in these graves was locally manufactured and appears to have been produced within a generally narrow chronological window.[135] Each contained at least one pouring vessel, at least one drinking cup, and at least one open bowl or dish. Two graves, Tomb 1 and Tomb 5, yielded examples of kyathoi of the relief ware class described above. Neither was originally inscribed, but stylistic traits of both suggest they belong to the northern class of this vessel form. These vessels, coupled with an example of a Proto-Corinthian aryballos also placed in Tomb 5, suggest that the date of these two burials fell within the period of the second quarter to the middle of the seventh century BCE. The typological correspondences of other ceramics from these two burials with those from the other seven burials of this group indicate that they should be dated to within the same approximate time frame.

This date also indicates that the individuals represented in these burials were likely alive around the period of transition between the Early Phase monumental domestic structure referred to as EPOC4 and the three buildings of the Intermediate Phase complex. However, the scale of materiality within the burials does not suggest that these individuals were residents of OC1/Residence. Burials of truly monumental scale consistent with the monumental houses of any of Poggio Civitate's stages of architectural development were either long ago lost to casual looting or have yet to be identified.

The overall arrangement of these burials indicates a ritual practice consistent with a broader, regional set of behaviors. The inclusion of pouring vessels, drinking cups, and plates or bowls is clearly an expression of a widely held funerary belief expressing the idea of a meal associated with the dead. This theme is present within Etruscan burials from the tenth or eleventh century BCE onward, and remains a fixture of funerary behaviors well after these Poggio Aguzzo burials. The wrapping of objects in textiles is also a common, if less well recognized, behavior associated with widely held burial rituals.[136] This behavior demonstrates that while the individuals represented by this group of burials from Poggio Aguzzo may not have been linked to the highest echelons of the community's leadership, they were recognized and honored in death according to commonly held precepts of collective behavior. Their bodies were wrapped and carried from Poggio Civitate to Poggio Aguzzo. A place of burial was excavated and prepared for each of them, and they were carefully laid within them along with the rudimentary material requirements needed to represent a meal. In short, they were recognized as members of a community that knew them in life and mourned them in death.

This was not true for everyone at Poggio Civitate. Recent analysis of bones collected over the decades of excavation at the site has revealed a number of perinatal human remains. In total, forty-two examples of fragments of these infant skeletal remains have been found, and in every case, the remains are recovered among high concentrations of other forms of debris. In no case is there evidence of any form of ritualized treatment of these perinatal human remains.[137] Instead, the current state of evidence suggests that infants who either were stillborn or failed to survive the early days or weeks of life were simply discarded with other forms of household debris.

This treatment of perinatal humans hints at social rituals that are usually less visible to the archaeological process. Obviously, various forms of ritual behaviors linked to the maturation process are known in other cultures, but among the Etruscans of this period we can be confident of little. Perhaps this treatment of perinatal human remains reflects customs wherein the naming and/or fuller acknowledgment of newly born children occurred at a prescribed point sometime after birth, when families were more confident of the survival of the infant.

Before the Fire

Evidence from OC2/Workshop's floor suggests that the community was in the planning stages of a new architectural project.[138] The unfired cover tiles resting on the building's floor, along with the similarly unfired revetment plaques, both indicate that another building was anticipated. The mold used to produce the male antefix type may have also played a role in this planning, even if evidence suggests the form was already in use at the time of the fire.

Moreover, a few curious materials, both from OC2/Workshop's floor and from across the plateau, suggest that the structure of the building that would replace Poggio Civitate's Intermediate Complex was already forming in the minds of the community's patrons and their artisans. For example, a fragment of a human figurine was recovered from the floor of OC2/Workshop (fig. 3.62).[139] This terracotta object preserves portions of the representation of a human arm, broken in such a manner as to indicate that it orig-

3.62. Terracotta figurine fragments

inally extended outward from the figure's torso. The hand grips a curved, horn-like object. Another terracotta object, recovered from Piano del Tesoro's northern flank, preserves the representation of a pair of feet shod in pointed shoes, resting on a squared platform (fig. 3.62).[140]

Both of these examples of small-scale human figurines closely anticipate the forms of several human akroteria associated with the site's Archaic Phase building, discussed in the following chapters. So while the fire appears to have been accidental, it is conceivable that at the time it occurred members of the community were already thinking of an ambitious building project that would radically reimagine the scale of elite domestic architecture at Poggio Civitate.

◦ 4 ◦
Monumental Aspirations

POGGIO CIVITATE'S ARCHAIC PHASE

(ca. 600 BCE to Approximately 525 BCE)

Following the fire that destroyed Poggio Civitate's Intermediate Phase, builders and architects reenvisioned the idea of a domestic structure, combining the separate elements of the buildings of the previous stage to form a single edifice (plan 3). The result was a building of massive scale. Four wings, each approximately 60 m in length, surrounded a partially colonnaded courtyard, an architectural form similar, if considerably larger than, to a contemporaneous structure at Roselle near the mouth of the Ombrone River.[1] Foundations consisted of dry masonry mostly comprising local limestone (fig. 4.1).

In addition to having four wings, the structure was fortified. Projecting from near the southwestern corner was a massive wall, partially preserved today to a height of up to 2.5 m.[2] This wall extended the western façade by an additional 30 m and was paralleled approximately 1.2 m to the west by a low wall preserved to a height of approximately 0.90 m. The foundations of a small room, 4.5 by 5 m in area, may indicate a guardhouse, although some scholars have advanced the possibility that these foundations served as a platform or otherwise elevated watchtower. At the opposite— northeastern—corner lies a similarly sized set of foundations, although without the defensive wall or sentry's path. Nevertheless, several scholars have suggested that both served as lookouts associated with the building's defense.[3]

The structure's defensive works turned at the southwestern corner of the Piano del Tesoro plateau and ran an additional 22 m along the plateau's southern edge, partially enclosing a well located to the south of the building's southern wing. However, this wall abruptly ends at the point where it reaches the remains of OC2/Workshop, apparently never completed.

Some evidence suggests that these fortifications were added after the building's initial construction, although how long after is difficult to determine.[4] The incomplete state of the southern defensive wall further suggests that the process of enclosing the southern area of the plateau occurred very late in the life of the building. It is possible that the debris remaining in the area from OC2/Workshop was simply piled up to discourage approach from that side of the hill. But if this is the case, it would suggest a hurried effort to secure the area, as such a rough and inelegant solution is not in keeping with the overall quality and sensibility of the building's architecture.

Moreover, two wells identified to the west of the structure both appear to have been constructed and used only very briefly before

4.1. View of Archaic Phase building, exposed western flank, during the 1969 excavation season

the building's final demolition.[5] This interest in the creation of new water sources might suggest that the population at the top of the hill suddenly expanded at a point in time synchronous with the construction of the defensive works. If so, the final architectural form of the building, with its various defensive features, seems to point to a growing insecurity among the building's inhabitants; as subsequent evidence detailed below would indicate, their concern was justified.

Upon its initial completion, Poggio Civitate's monumental structure, dating to the years between the beginning of the sixth century BCE and the final third to end of the same century, would have been a sight to behold. Numerous details of the building's form remain necessarily speculative, but the state of preserved evidence allows for a considerable degree of informed speculation as to its appearance (fig. 4.2).

Precisely how the rooflines of the building's wings intersected is not certain. Nowhere at the site do we see evidence of valley tiles that would signal an impluvium-style intersection.[6] Given the absence of evidence on this point, most reconstructions of the building imagine different elevations associated with the four wings.[7] This solution would allow ridgepoles of three wings to intersect with elements of perpendicular walls, while seams created by the abutting roofing tiles of these three sides could have been infilled with plaster. Several preserved details of the building's northern wing suggest it was the tallest of the four wings. Its interior is subdivided into four chambers of variable size, and overall it is considerably larger in area than the other three wings, with walls that are somewhat more robust in width. Moreover, excavation of this wing revealed indications of postholes placed at regular intervals along the interior walls of the north and south sides of the wing. The curious widening of the northern foundation wall at its eastern extent may represent an ancient repair to the foundations. Both the original width of the foundations and the presence of a timber infrastructure within this wing suggest a higher roofline. Therefore, many reconstructions posit that the rooflines of the eastern and

4.2. Reconstruction of the Archaic Phase building, viewed from the southeast

western wings of the building were designed to meet the wall of the northern flank at a point lower than the northern flank's roof. If so, we might envision the southern flank's roof at an elevation equal to that of the northern flank, or at an elevation lower still than that of the eastern and western flanks, as is presumed in figure 4.2.

As mentioned above, the interior space of the building's northern wing is divided into four separate spaces. The opposite, southern wing is both narrower in width and divided into seven interior spaces of variable size. The eastern and westernmost rooms of the southern wing are shared by the eastern and western wings respectively, and are equal to each other in their dimensions. The eastern wing was originally constructed on top of bedrock, and little survives to describe its form other than the single surviving room shared with the southern wing and fragmentary elements of walls that project from the northern wing. However, the western wing is well preserved and consists of a series of rooms of differing sizes. The northern and southernmost rooms (shared with the northern and southern wings) are slightly larger than the four rooms of approximately equal size between them. The central space of this wing appears to have been left open, creating a three-walled space. Immediately to the east of this space is a curious squared enclosure. The walls of this enclosure are considerably less robust than those of the structure itself. While it is possible these foundations supported a wattle-and-daub wall or screen of some form, their purpose remains unclear.[8]

Clusters of small stones packed into circular formations and spaced at regular intervals along the southern, eastern, and northern flanks of the courtyard indicate that a loggia ran around these sides of the building's interior. The absence of the loggia along the western flank, coupled with the unusual squared enclosure, might suggest that this area and the squared enclosure served a function of some social or ritual distinction, but no other evidence supports this supposition.

Two additional buildings stood in immediate proximity to the northern and southern flanks respectively. The northern structure was the larger of the two, with foundation walls of approximately 0.75 m in width and interior walling that divided the space into three rooms of unequal size. The structure to the south was considerably more gracile, with thin foundations of only one or two registers of fieldstones. While some scholars have suggested the southern foundation stones could have supported a terracotta roof, this seems unlikely.[9] The difference in this foundation's construction technique from that of contemporary structures may indicate that it supported a thatched or similar non-rigid covering. Alternatively, it is possible the area was unroofed and served as a pen or enclosure for animals.

Stratigraphic evidence indicates that these two buildings were constructed later than the Intermediate Phase Complex, although their chronological relationship to the Archaic Phase building is less clear. Some scholars, preferring to see the Archaic Phase building standing in isolation, have advanced the possibility that these two buildings represent a temporary phase of housing built prior to the construction of the Archaic Phase building. It is equally possible that the northern and southern structures were contemporaneous with some portion or all of the life cycle of the Archaic Phase building.

Excavation records detail the remnants of an eclectic range of differing wall construction techniques. Some mud brick was seen at the time of excavation, still resting on elements of foundation walls and primarily preserved along the building's western flank.[10] Elsewhere, evidence of the use of pisé, a process of sequentially layering and lightly firing layered clay, is documented in various areas of the building.[11] Moreover, a considerable quantity of daub pieces preserving indications of wattle suggests that this form of walling was also used.

But regardless of the specific form of walling used in different areas of the building, the overall structure was robust enough to support a roof that consisted of the standard pan- and cover-tile arrangement complemented by numerous types of terracotta decorative ornaments. When viewed as a coherent whole, the iconographic program of the building can be understood as communicating themes related to aristocratic identity and authority.

The Decorative System of Poggio Civitate's Archaic Phase Building

The decorative program of Poggio Civitate's Archaic Phase building was constructed of local clay tempered with heat-treated, crushed limestone. This distinctive terracotta is often referred to as "Murlo terracotta."[12] Recent elemental testing of clay sources indicates that the clay beds exploited were located on the hill to the west of Piano del Tesoro.

Some elements, such as the rooftop akroteria and the feline figures of the lateral sima, were partially drawn from molds and then hand-formed. Indeed, the interior surfaces of most examples of terracotta sculpture preserve finger impressions where the artisans pressed clay into matrices, while outer surfaces often preserve fingerprints from smoothing and working.[13] Other decorative items, such as the frieze plaques, gorgon antefixes, and female appliqués of the lateral sima, employed matrices that allowed for reasonably quick replication of the decorative forms required by the considerable size of the building. One fragment of such a matrix was recovered during excavation. This mold, for the production of the female appliqué of the lateral sima, was recovered to the west of Piano del Tesoro, suggesting that industrial or working areas may have been located in this area (fig. 4.3).[14]

Antefixes in the form of gorgons decorated the building's exterior. Each plaque was affixed to a terminal cover tile and rested directly on the eaves (fig. 4.4).[15] As with much of the terracotta decoration of this building, a considerable number of these gorgon antefixes were recovered from a large deposition to the west of the building. However, geospatial plotting of examples of these plaques and their fragments shows a general pattern of distribution that strongly suggests that they ornamented the building's exterior perimeter. In addition to these gorgon antefixes, a considerably

4.3. Mold for female appliqué of the Archaic lateral sima

4.4. Gorgon antefix, obverse and reverse

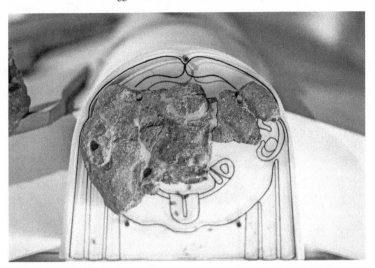

4.5. Columen plaque in form of gorgon

larger image of a gorgon was recovered.[16] This larger gorgon was perforated with a series of nail holes, supporting the conclusion that it served as a decorative columen plaque covering a projecting wooden surface of a ridgepole beam—and thus would have been visible from the building's exterior (fig. 4.5).[17]

The eaves of the interior courtyard were adorned with a sculpted lateral sima (fig. 4.6). This decorative element consisted of a typical pantile with one end bounded by a high wall surmounted by a curved, strigilated molding. The wall was perforated slightly to the left of its center with a spout for water, which was channeled down the space between two registers of cover tiles. The exterior portion of this spout was shaped into the form of a feline.[18] Two circular rosettes flanked the waterspout, and the rightmost side of the sima's wall was ornamented with an appliqué in the form of a female head. The back of each female appliqué was partially scored and half was adhered to the sima wall, allowing the other half of the head to overlap with the adjacent sima element.[19] Some fragments of the front portion of the lateral simae preserve traces of a painted

4.6. Archaic Phase lateral sima and reconstruction

key meander pattern that was rendered on the underside of the tile and would thus have been visible from below (fig. 4.7).[20]

Like the lateral sima, the raking sima consisted of an otherwise ordinary pantile with one augmented side. This augmented side was crowned by a curved, strigilated molding similar to that of the lateral sima. Below this molding was a decorative relief consisting of repeating images of dogs chasing rabbits or hares (fig. 4.8).[21]

The sculptures that adorned the building's roof are among the more evocative and enigmatic images in the existing corpus of Etruscan iconography. Each was attached directly to ridgepole tiles and produced by a combination of molds and hand modeling. The

4.7. Underside of lateral sima with painted meander

4.8. Archaic Phase raking sima

4.9. Bearded male
akroterion

various figures were assembled from separately formed elements
that were joined before firing.[22] These enthroned human figures
are the images that have been most widely associated with Poggio Civitate since the early years of the excavation project (fig. 4.9).
Based on a count of extant representations of hands, feet, and other
elements of the sculptures, at least fifteen such figures were present
on the roof.[23] Several male figures have squared beards, while others are beardless. Preserved portions of some torso fragments, as
well as examples rendered at a smaller scale, indicate that some of
the figures depicted females (fig. 4.10). Composite estimates based
on more intact, fragmentary examples suggest that the largest of
the enthroned figures were approximately 1.5 m tall.[24]

The seated figures seem to have originally held some form of at-
tribute. The larger male figures held ornaments positioned horizon-

4.10. Female enthroned akroterion

tally across their laps. Conversely, the hands of smaller, apparently female figures appear to have been positioned vertically. The original attributes, whatever they were, were likely produced in wood or some other medium that has not survived. The seated and standing figures frieze plaque type, discussed below, may offer relief representations of the kind of attributes these images originally held.[25]

These figures wore gowns and pointed shoes, and some preserve elements of red and white paint employed to enhance the designs. Surviving paint suggests the hems of garments were decorated with a meander pattern while the shoes were complimented with a tongue pattern (fig. 4.11).[26] Each enthroned figure sat on a squared, straight-legged stool.

Perhaps the most distinctive element of these statues was the headdresses worn by some. At least three figures wore helmets,

4.11. Enthroned human
figure with painted
design

of various forms, although it is not possible to determine whether
these helmets were depicted on standing or seated figures. Conversely, others wore a headdress that featured a broad brim with a
high, pointed crown. No direct parallel for this type of headgear
has yet to emerge in the corpus of Etruscan iconography. However,
high-crowned, brimmed hats are seen on representations of human figures on situlae (buckets) from the region of the Veneto,[27]
and a smaller version of a peaked hat is depicted hanging from the
edge of a tent awning in the frescoes from Tarquinia's Tomb of the
Hunter.[28] The Poggio Civitate figures' hats wide brims and distinctive crowns may simply have been a local innovation.[29] Nevertheless, their remarkable form encouraged a scholar no less than
Ranucchio Bianchi Bandinelli to dub the sculptures "Cowboy"
statues, a moniker that has tenaciously clung to these remarkable
and curious figures.[30]

At least some of the human figures on the rooftop were depicted standing. Four examples of ridgepole tiles preserve attached representations of shod feet, indicating that there were at least three standing figures.[31] One example preserves the feet and legs of a figure in an apparent *knielauf*, or rapid motion, position, perhaps indicating that they were originally associated not with human figures but rather with fantastic creatures such as gorgons, with which this pose is frequently associated in Greek iconography (fig. 4.12).[32]

Because the sculptures were attached to ridgepole tiles, they could have been placed anywhere along the roof's peak. Several fragments recovered along the building's northern and western flanks suggest that those wings displayed the seated figures. However, numerous other fragments of the figures were recovered within depositions located to the west of the building, in trenches called Civitate A2 and Civitate A24. As a result, it is not possible to determine whether the images adorned specific wings of the building or encircled it entirely. Indeed, it is not even possible to know whether they faced inward toward the courtyard or outward toward the surrounding area.

4.12. Figure in *knielauf* pose

4.13. Sphinx akroterion

Study of the animal akroteria fragments indicates that a range of creatures was represented: sphinxes (fig. 4.13), horses, hippocamps, griffons, boars, rams, lions, bovines, and at least one possible centaur.[33] The various preserved animal paws and hooves bear indications that they were positioned laterally along the length of their associated ridgepole tiles, permitting them to be viewed and fully interpreted from either within or outside the building (figs. 4.14–17).[34] However, while their location on the roof is clear, the specific placement of the images and their relationship to the standing and seated human figures is impossible to determine with any confidence. It is tempting to imagine that the animal figures were positioned on either side of each human image, creating a heraldic presentation echoing the iconography of divinity represented on the building's lateral sima (discussed below), but the available evidence does not permit certainty on this point.

Four types of frieze plaque also ornamented areas of the building. Each is approximately 54 cm in length and, when intact, was

4.14. Sphinx akroterion fragment, front view

4.15. Animal hindquarter akroterion fragment

4.16. Boar head akroterion fragment

4.17. Horse akroterion fragment

4.18. Horse-race frieze plaque and painted reconstruction

perforated by five regularly spaced nail holes, which allowed it to be attached to wooden beams or similar surfaces. Each plaque is also crowned by a squared, strigilated cavetto molding beneath which there is a pattern of twenty-two dentils of alternating eleva-tion. The lowest portion of each plaque displays a simple guilloche pattern, forming the groundline for the four different scene types.

One type consists of a scene of horse racing (fig. 4.18).[35] Read from left to right, the first image is of a large cauldron on an orna-mental stand. Three horse and rider groups move from left to right, away from the cauldron. Each rider is identical to the rest, with a peaked cap, a flowing cape, and a riding crop in the left hand and reins in the right. The front hooves of the two rear horses are raised, as if in mid-gallop, while those of the lead horse are close to the groundline of the guilloche border. All three horses are depicted with flowing manes.

Numerous examples of all four of Poggio Civitate's frieze plaque types—along with an enormous quantity of the building's other ornamentation—were recovered in a concentrated grouping located west of the building. This deposit, identified by trenches excavated in the area where they were located as "Civitate A2" and "Civitate A24," lay in a depression, perhaps intentionally excavated, into which a considerable amount of architectural debris was then discarded, a phenomenon discussed on the pages that follow.[36] However, examples of the horse-race frieze plaque recovered beyond this specific deposition clearly cluster along the western flank of the Archaic Phase building, suggesting that this scene ornamented that side of the building.

A second plaque type depicts a scene of banqueting (fig. 4.19).[37] This scene shows pairs of figures reclining on two couches. Be-

4.19. Banquet frieze plaque and painted reconstruction

4.20. Procession frieze plaque and painted reconstruction

tween the couches is a finely wrought stand supporting a cauldron. Servants attend the banqueters, one of whom plays a lyre. Beneath both couches are tables laden with vessels containing food. Under the tables are dogs, prepared to enjoy scraps that might fall to them from the meal.

Like the horse-race frieze plaque, the banquet scene was also heavily represented in the Civitate A2 and Civitate A24 areas. However, examples that were not recovered from that deposit show a clear concentration along the northern flank of the Archaic Phase building, suggesting that this wing of the Archaic Phase structure was ornamented with this scene.

A third plaque type depicts a scene of a procession (fig. 4.20).[38] Unlike the horse-race and seated figures scenes (to be discussed below), the pictorial orientation of this scene moves from right to left.

On the left side of the scene, two identical figures holding staves lead a pair of horses hitched to a cart. The inner horse is depicted with one front hoof raised, while the outer horse has both front hoofs on the ground. The cart hitched to the horses consists of a platform resting on two wheels, shaded by a parasol. Two human figures are seated beneath the parasol, the one in the foreground wearing a mantle that covers the head, indicating this figure is female. Two additional figures stand behind the cart. Both carry fans, and the leftmost of the two also carries a cista on the head. The final figure on the plaque balances a curious, square-legged object on the head. This object, discussed below, is an important key to understanding the interrelated meaning of all four plaques and their relationship to the building's entire decorative program.

The procession scene is not as well preserved as either the horse-race or banquet plaque types. However, if the examples recovered from within the Civitate A2 and Civitate A24 deposits are excluded from consideration, the geospatial distribution of examples of this type concentrate along the southern flank of the Archaic Phase building.

The fourth plaque type depicts a series of seated and standing figures, all facing to the right (fig. 4.21).[39] The rightmost is a bearded male seated on a campstool. His feet rest on an ornamental footrest and in his right hand he holds a lituus, an item representative of religious authority in Etruscan and later Roman sociopolitical environments. Behind him stands a figure holding a sword and a spear. Next is a female, seated on a cylindrical throne as her feet rest on an ornamental footrest.[40] In her right hand she holds a flower, while her left opens her veil outward, revealing her face. Behind her, in the center of the scene, is a standing attendant holding a fan and a situla. Three seated figures appear behind the central attendant. The bearded male in the center of this group holds a double axe while the two females beside him hold flowers.

Given the geospatial distribution of the banquet scene in the north, the horse-race in the west, and the procession in the south, it is reasonable to conclude that the seated and standing figures

4.21. Seated and standing figures frieze plaque and painted reconstruction

scene ornamented the eastern wing of the Archaic Phase building
(fig. 4.22). However, virtually all examples of this plaque type were
recovered within the Civitate A2 and A24 deposits to the west.
The curiously thorough treatment on this specific plaque suggests
its image communicated something of particular importance to
the individuals who dismantled and destroyed this structure during the final years of the sixth century BCE, a possibility explored
below.

Interpreting the Archaic Phase Decorative Program

While the various portions of Poggio Civitate's Archaic Phase decorative program have been extensively studied, these analyses tend
to consider individual ornamental elements in isolation from one

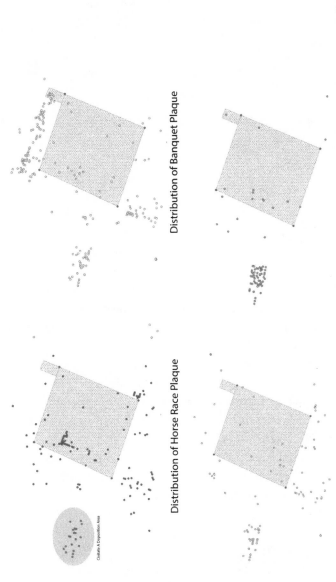

Distribution of Horse Race Plaque

Distribution of Banquet Plaque

Distribution of Procession Plaque

Distribution of Seated and Standing Figures Plaque

Cistiaie A Deposition Area

4.22. Distribution of frieze plaque types

4.23. Archaic roof reconstruction

another. When considered together, the interrelated iconographic elements convey a coherent and sophisticated message of elite authority, identity, and prestige (fig. 4.23).

The four frieze plaque types can be understood and read sequentially. The procession scene, with its depiction of a woman beneath a mantle, is quite likely a representation of the arrival of a bride and her retinue to the community. The two figures following the cart carry fans in their right hands and situlae or braziers in their left. Fans are a feature of several elite burials of the seventh century BCE in both Etruria and Latium.[41] Therefore, these items were likely markers of social status in central Italy, as they were in Egypt and the Near East, although in Italy they appear more closely and specifically linked to the status of women.[42] However, Poggio Civitate's fan bearers also carry objects balanced on their heads, indicating they represent attendants, servants, or enslaved persons and the fans are for the benefit of the individuals on the cart.

The objects carried atop the heads of these two figures are instructive. The leftmost of the two carries a cylindrical container on his or her head. While clearly such a container could be employed to carry any number of things, it is noteworthy that a frequently depicted function of such vessels is to hold wool. Several representations from the Greek world depicting women engaged in the act of spinning and weaving show cylindrical vessels, called *ciste*, containing the carded wool that is drawn out during the fiber spinning process.

The object carried on the head of the rightmost rear figure is slightly more problematic. Gantz suggests the figure carries a folding campstool of a type employed by four of the five seated figures on the seated figures frieze plaque.[43] However, depictions of figures carrying such folding seats elsewhere in the corpus of Etruscan iconography—such as the small figure appearing in the corner of the right wall of Tarquinia's Tomb of the Augurs[44]—show that artisans interested in showing such objects would naturally show the curve of the stool's legs, which the Poggio Civitate image does not. Instead, two spoked elements are stacked on top of one another. Each spoke ends with a notch at its top. If Poggio Civitate's artisans wished to represent a folded campstool, this is probably not how they would have done so.

Instead, a more likely candidate for the object carried by the final attendant is a yarn swift (fig. 4.24).[45] These objects typically consist of four notched spokes around which spun yarn is wound, and can be folded in a manner akin to that depicted on the frieze.[46] Yarn swifts are used to facilitate the stringing of a loom's warp or to help with winding yarn hanks into balls or other portable forms. If the final attendant of this scene carries such an object, a natural complement to the cista carried by the individual immediately to the left, a clearer picture of the scene's implicit narrative emerges. The activities of weaving and textile production were a standard feature of ancient households, and a form of production most frequently connected to women.[47] Whether in the mythological character of Penelope or in any number of later representations of women and weaving, explicit connections between the domestic sphere, the act of textile production, and female socio-sexual virtue are clear.[48] The loom provided men the ability to leave the household, return at

4.24. Modern four-
spoked yarn swift

a time that suited them, and see the evidence of a wife's continued presence within the household expressed progressively through the emerging textile. In aristocratically organized political communities, an overriding concern for patrilineal legitimacy of one's heirs often results in social structures designed to control and limit female sexual behavior.

If we are correct in our interpretation of the ciste and possible yarn swift carried by the rear attendants of the procession, the procession scene as a whole can be plausibly interpreted as depicting the arrival of a bride into a new household, bringing with her the material instruments reflective of her "virtue." It is similarly noteworthy that the foremost of the two figures seated on the scene's cart wears a mantle that covers most of the head and body. While we cannot identify this figure with total confidence, the gesture of a similar figure appearing on Poggio Civitate's seated figures plaque (discussed below) supports the interpretation that this figure in the procession scene is the bride, arriving at her new home.

If the procession scene is depicting a bride's arrival to her new home, the banquet and horse-race scenes can be understood as complementing this narrative. Episodic celebratory events are difficult to see in Poggio Civitate's material record. However, a few bits of evidence hint at periodic spikes in the production that may be associated with such behavior.[49]

As discussed earlier, simple glyphs in the form of letters or non-alphabetic symbols are occasionally placed on pottery—some prior to firing, some after. These glyphs, or *sigla*, only appear on a very small percentage of ceramics from the site, although similar glyphs are found on examples of pottery from nearly every Etruscan settlement in the region.[50] Marking pottery in this manner bears similarities to the process of marking roofing materials described earlier. If episodic spikes in the production of a range of ceramics were required, it is appealing to imagine that different groups would mark contributions with indications of the wares for which they were responsible. Some such events would have been seasonally predictable, such as harvest festivals. Others, such as birthday celebrations—assuming such matters concerned the Etruscans—or important anniversaries would have been similarly predictable. Other events requiring broader community action may have been ad hoc concerns: births of social importance, funerals, military celebrations, and, of course, marriages.

Moreover, at least one inscribed figurine from Poggio Civitate's Intermediate Phase OC1/Residence appears to directly demonstrate a connection between the site and another community. On the reverse of this example (fig. 4.25), there are portions of an inscription that can be reconstructed as the name *[vh]astia kilan[aia].*[51] This family name is attested around the region of Arezzo and potentially indicates the movement of a woman from that community and *gens* group into that of Poggio Civitate.[52]

While neither the corpus of *sigla* nor the single inscribed name of a potentially Arretine woman is conclusive, marriage between elite families of different communities was a likely feature of aristocratic life in Etruscan communities of this period. This ritualized form of population exchange would probably consist of young, marriageable women moving between communities, and one such incidence of this is depicted by the mantled figure on the cart of the procession frieze.

Therefore, if the *sigla* found on certain classes of pottery were related to episodic celebratory events requiring additional materials, the tablewares on which they are found indicate that one feature of

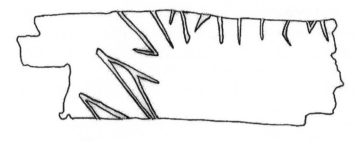

4.25. Figurine fragment with *[vh]astia kilan[aia]* inscription from OC1/ Residence

such an event would be large-scale, public banqueting. If so, and if the procession plaque does represent an arrival of the bride scene, the representation on the banquet plaque, a scene in which male and female figures recline together on the same couch, is reasonably construed as a marriage feast.

In keeping with this theme, images of spectacles and sporting events involving horses are also well known within the Etruscan sphere. Although later in date and more closely associated with funerary environments, images of chariot racing or horseback riding are found in several painted tombs of the sixth century BCE.[53] Such scenes suggest that athletic spectacles involving horses were features of grandiose events connected to elite funerary behavior of the Archaic period. As a result, it is not difficult to imagine that similar kinds of prestigious events would have also marked celebrations of a non-funerary nature.

The fourth frieze plaque, the seated and standing figures image, explicitly represents the notion of elite identity and its essential connection to intermarriage between elite families. The bearded male figure, seated at the rightmost side of the scene, holds a lituus, a symbol widely recognized in the Italic sphere and connected to religious authority. The lituus is connected to religious identity within the social aristocracy, and appears in a number of Etruscan contexts, including Tarquinia's Tomb of the Augurs.[54] It accompanies the figure recovered from the area of Asciano's Molinello Tumulus,[55] and an actual example of a lituus was recovered from a Cerveteri burial of the Archaic period;[56] there are numerous representations of the object from the later Roman world.

On the plaque, another figure, holding a sword and spear, stands behind this male figure. The items he holds suggest that this figure is not a mere slave but rather an arms bearer associated with the lituus-holding male.[57] The interrelationship between religious and military authority further reinforces the status of the foremost seated figure. The female figure seated on the cylindrical throne opens her veil. This gesture is one that is immediately recognizable and associated with brides.[58] Therefore, we can plausibly imagine that the three additional seated figures on the left side of the scene represent that family now enlarged by the addition of the bride.

Therefore, the four plaques may be read sequentially. The procession scene depicts the arrival of an unmarried woman from outside the community. Her attendants carry textile production equipment that she will employ to set up a loom within the household of her future husband, expressive of her female virtue and worthiness to join the Poggio Civitate household. The event of the marriage is celebrated with convivial feasting, represented in the banquet plaque. Horse racing further reinforces the public spectacle of the event, an ostentatious display of the power and opulence of the family that welcomes the woman to her new household. The seated and standing figures frieze represents the bride amongst her new family. We need not imagine that a specific event is depicted by these repeating images; rather, they display a general theme appropriate for the overall architectural space, regardless of when the wedding in question occurred.[59]

In order to best experience the building's iconography, the viewer would have had to enter the structure either from the west or through an otherwise unpreserved doorway on the building's eastern façade. Once inside, the viewer standing beneath the loggia of the eastern, southern, or northern façades would perceive the lateral sima's painted underside with its repeating image of a female face flanked by felines and floral motifs that ran the length of the building's sides. As described earlier, the female surrounded by such iconographic elements is a widely represented concept throughout central Italy and represented an evolving concept of a fertility divinity. Such images were first seen in the region by the mid to late eighth century BCE, and were quickly adopted by local craftspeople acting at the behest of aristocratic patrons who wished to promote themes of fertility.[60] Should the viewer step a meter or two into the courtyard, this repeating image of a fertility divinity would serve as a visual foundation for the sculptures mounted onto the building's apex.

This arrangement raises a critical question: who or what is represented by the human figures ornamenting the building's roofline? While the figures wearing the broad-brimmed hats are certainly arresting, not every figure wears such a head ornament. Some appear to wear a form of helmet with a crowning pommel[61] (fig. 4.26), while one is depicted bareheaded with a fillet encircling his forehead (fig. 4.27).[62] In all likelihood, the attributes of the various figures assisted the ancient observer in interpreting the images.

The human figures could represent divinities, especially if the menagerie of various animal figures were positioned in a heraldic manner flanking the various human figures. However, without certainty as to where either the humans or animals were placed, this suggestion also must remain speculative. It is equally possible that the images were intended to represent the members of the family that inhabited the house itself—or the august and venerated ancestry of that family, an idea also consistent with the possibility of human figures flanked by animal images.

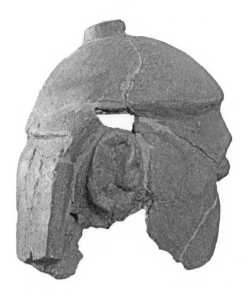

4.26. Human figure with helmet akroterion

4.27. Male with fillet akroterion

While the repeating imagery of the building's lateral sima was physically disconnected from the human figures placed above it on the structure's roofline, they would still have been visually associated with one another. Therefore, it is possible that the human figures on the rooftop were understood to represent divinities as well as ancestors of the family inhabiting the structure. Indeed, this specific ambiguity may have been entirely intentional. And if the ancient viewer confused the living members of an elite family with divinized or valorized ancestral figures, or imagined them to be the descendants of such divinity, so much the political better.

The building's exterior display of gorgoneia (the antefixes and columen plaques) and the images on the raking sima that apparently reference hunting are both also linked to themes of elite identity and prerogative. Hunting is typically characteristic of elite behavior.[63] Images of hunting are known in Etruscan iconography from the Iron Age onward, adorning a number of prestige objects, such as scabbards and ornamental bangles.[64] Direct evidence for the hunting of dangerous, large animals is clearly visible in the animal bone assemblage from OC1/Residence described above, even if the evidence for the hunting of animals such as the hares depicted on the raking sima tends to cluster within the industrial space of OC2/Workshop. Nevertheless, hunting would have been an elite activity occurring outside the household itself, creating the opportunity for publicly visible displays of valor and prestige while also providing surplus meat to the larger community.[65]

The image of the gorgon is a complicated one. Clearly, with fangs bared and eyes wide, the gorgon presents a defensive, malevolent gaze to the viewer. However, the gorgon is a figure that shared an iconographic language with that of the common expression of fertility divinities in central Italy and elsewhere. Images of gorgons flanked by felines or waterbirds, while not overly common, are found throughout the central and eastern Mediterranean, suggesting that some feature of this supernatural figure was understood to be connected to fertility, although precisely how is not clearly expressed in any surviving mythological narrative or iconographic source.[66]

The gorgon is a concept and narrative of monstrosity that emphasizes the creature's eyes. The gaze of the gorgon, even after its defeat and decapitation, remains a potent and powerful force. The gorgon mask in the form of the antefix redirects this gaze, focusing it outward to create a protective perimeter around the inhabitants of the structure. In this regard, the gorgon is an apotropaic device, an image or symbol that protects against evil. The symbolic interaction between the symbolic eye, or "malocchio" (i.e., vagina), and the horn, or "cornetto" (i.e., penis), is as evident in the Etruscan period as it remains today in modern Italy.[67] The symbolic implication is that when these forces are in balance, fertility and conception will follow. But when they are unbalanced by malevolent influences, infertility and impotence are the result.

The benevolent iteration of this concept is depicted on the building's interior. The lateral sima's repeating image of the Mistress of Animals is an iconographical scene drawn from eastern Mediterranean sources and incorporated into a number of material and ritual environments. The iconography clearly depicts a divinity connected to fertility, whether she was known as Ishtar, Astarte, Artemis, or, as is ultimately documented in the slightly later Etruscan sphere, Uni. From the concept's earliest adoption in Italy, it was most often connected with feline familiars and floral ornaments.[68] This divinity's prevalence throughout central Italy from the eighth century onward reflects the importance of fertility and procreation for families organized around principles of political inheritance. As political and social forms of central Italy became linked to inheritance and ideas of valorized ancestry,[69] members of emerging aristocratic families increasingly emphasized this type of divinity in funerary and non-funerary environments. Indeed, the Etruscans were early proponents of the practice of linking familial ancestry to a narrative of descent from precisely this type of fertility divinity.[70] Of equal importance was the projection of that authority and identity into the future by means of procreation. Sex and sexuality among members of the social aristocracy could be construed as, at least in part, a political act. The production of an heir, through

4.28. Reconstructed view of the Archaic Phase building, southern wing

the agency of the goddess associated with fertility, was nothing less than an existential concern for the family.

The akroterial sculptures were given the position of greatest prominence on the building and were the only element of the building's decorative program that would have been visible from both inside and outside the structure. At that angle, the viewer, looking up to the roof's apex, would see both the representation of the goddess of fertility and also images of the august family residing within. Whether this message was meant to represent the specific, living family or a more stylized description of the family's valorized ancestry, we cannot say. This connection is one of many examples of political propaganda seen throughout the Etruscan and Roman world, where members of elite families sought to connect themselves and their ancestry to narratives of generational descent from this type of goddess.[71]

Fertility is the fulcrum upon which balances the complementary concepts of ancestry and progeny. For members of Poggio Civitate's aristocracy, as with almost any aristocracy, parental legitimacy was a driving concern within the community's political equation. The frieze plaque series depicting various aspects of matrimonial events can be said to illustrate this concern. The thematically interconnected scenes of a bride's arrival, a marriage feast, celebratory games to mark and elevate the occasion, and finally, the image of the resulting family all illustrate this concept. The gorgons of the building's exterior and Mistress of Animals images of the interior's lateral sima represent facets of the divinity essential to elite marriage—the goddess responsible for fertility and reproduction. Finally, atop the building are human and animal figures, visually linked to this goddess and connecting the inhabitants to the divine source of their authority (fig. 4.28). In this manner, the ruling family of Poggio Civitate communicated their power and identity to those who looked up to them from below.

The Function(s) of Poggio Civitate's Archaic Phase Building

The nature of Poggio Civitate's ultimate destruction makes detailed questions concerning the functions of various areas of this building difficult to ascertain. Other than fragmentary debris associated with the building's decoration, very little material evidence pointing to the function and purpose of different spaces within the structure was recovered over the course of excavation. However, a few clues do suggest possible uses of some areas.

For example, the evidence for large-scale, communal banqueting seen in association with Poggio Civitate's Intermediate Phase shows that the community periodically engaged in such events. If communal banqueting was a feature of activities within the Archaic Phase building, it is likely that such events occurred within the area of the building's northern wing (fig. 4.29). Not only is the westernmost room of this wing the largest within the entire structure, but the geospatial distribution of fragments of the banquet frieze plaque clearly cluster within this area. Of course, other forms

4.29. Hypothetical banquet hall scene

of gatherings could have occurred there, whether social, legal, or political. It is equally easy to imagine that the building's courtyard served as a place for large gatherings if the nature of such events required even more room for invitees to gather.

Fragments of a stone altar, the majority of which was recovered within a well (described below), were recovered in the area immediately south of the building's southern wall. Perhaps tellingly, this is the approximate area originally occupied by the Intermediate Phase OC3/Tripartite structure, a building that, as argued earlier, served some form of religious function. If an altar were originally located in this part of the building, it would logically follow that some form of religious activity was centered in this area (fig. 4.30).

Unfortunately, the absence of material evidence for other purposes associated with the building, coupled with the damage by erosion to approximately 75 percent of the building's eastern wing, make even speculative guesses as to various functions difficult. Clearly, living quarters would have been necessary, although no specific area would be obviously better suited for such use than any other.

Of course, a structure as curious as Poggio Civitate's Archaic Phase building has attracted the attention of many scholars over the years. The site's original excavator, Kyle Meredith Phillips, first tentatively described the structure as a sanctuary. However, as evidence from the site accrued, Phillips's interpretation became more cautious. His ultimate suggestion—that the building served as a meeting hall associated with a political league—did not enjoy the benefit of subsequent evidence pointing to features of the site's larger community.[72] Cristofani's contemporary counterargument pointed to the building's scale and ornamentation and suggested that it served as a palazzo.[73] Cristofani was quick to note that the nuanced meaning of "palazzo" in Italian did not entirely

4.30. Hypothetical festival within the Archaic Phase courtyard

correspond to its English translation and could embrace a number of functions beyond simply that of an elite residence. Since that
time, other scholars have offered various interpretive possibilities.
Edlund-Berry envisions a domestic function beyond Phillip's suggestion of a meeting hall.[74] Turfa and Steinmayer note the similarities between the structure and some features of defensive forts of
colonial America, suggesting a keep or fortress.[75] De Grummond,
emphasizing the large open space of the building's courtyard, has
suggested it served as a kind of forum for the community.[76]

In the broader social context of aristocratic behavior and identity of the Etruscan Archaic period, these explanations for the
building's form need not be viewed as mutually exclusive. That the
space served as an elite domicile seems evident from its relationship to the earlier OC1/Residence and the preceding review of the
structure's ornamental program. However, as is evident even in
elite domestic architecture of the site's earliest phase (the EPOC4
structure of the early Orientalizing period), the building's form allows for a degree of large-scale gathering. Within EPOC4's front
porch, the visible, semi-public space could easily have been used
for small gatherings, communal banquets, and other similar activities. The indications of larger-scale communal banqueting described above and associated with the site's Intermediate Phase
OC1/Residence suggest that as the community grew, this feature
of elite behavior increased in scale as well. Therefore, the idea of a
semi-public gathering space within the Archaic Phase building is
entirely in keeping with the community's earlier stages of development.[77] Similarly, the possibility that such gatherings involved individuals from communities of the wider region around Poggio Civitate is possible as well. Thus, Phillips's original suggestion of the
structure as a social and political gathering space or meeting hall
remains plausible, although perhaps not in quite as regionally ex-
pansive a form as he and some others may have envisioned.[78]

Moreover, a gathering body of evidence suggests that communities similar to Poggio Civitate were present on hilltops throughout the area. From Piano Tondo near Castelnuovo Berardenga, ar-

eas excavated in 1978 revealed traces of a structure employing a tiled, terracotta roof.[79] Within this roofing debris were several examples of decorative antefixes in the form of female heads similar to those of Poggio Civitate's Intermediate Phase. Fragments of simple impasto, bucchero, and depurated wares were also recovered in this deposit. While the remains from Castelnuovo Berardenga are modest in comparison to the volume of material preserved from Poggio Civitate, they indicate that a building with a decoratively similar sensibility was located at another community visible from Poggio Civitate.

Traces of a large rectilinear structure have also recently come to light at the site of Orgia, on the Merse River to the east of Poggio Civitate.[80] While excavation and study of this potentially similar structure are needed before any comparison to Poggio Civitate is possible, it is inviting to imagine that other similarly organized communities were located throughout the area, controlling territories and populations through similar mechanisms of social and iconographic display.

The Destruction and Abandonment of Poggio Civitate

The latest pottery recovered from stratified deposits at Poggio Civitate are fragments of Laconian III pottery associated with the Hunt Painter and dated to the years around the third quarter of the sixth century BCE.[81] This material provides a general sense of when the site was destroyed and abandoned and that, in turn, might help explain why.

Activities preceding the settlement's destruction appear to indicate a degree of concern over security. Relevant here are the two wells located west of Piano del Tesoro, mentioned above.[82] Both were simple, stone-lined constructions that reached groundwater at a depth of approximately 3.5 to 4 m (fig. 4.31). Both also appear to have been used for a very brief period of time.

The excavation of one of these wells, located a few meters west of the southwestern corner of the Archaic Phase building's defensive

4.31. Well after excavation

4.32. 1979 excavation of corner of sentry's path with sling stones

works, produced a stratigraphic section revealing that elements of the building's decorative scheme were damaged at or near the time of the well's construction. Fragments of one of the exterior gorgon antefixes that were recovered from the well's construction trench indicate that some architectural debris was in the area to the southwest of the building while it was still standing.[83]

One explanation for the presence of architectural debris within the fill of a well construction that predates the destruction of the Archaic Phase building is as follows: the building's southwestern corner was augmented with the construction of a defensive work. This effort consisted of the pair of walls described earlier that met the building's southwest corner. The westernmost wall rose to the height of about 1 m, approximately that of a person's waist. The interior wall was considerably higher and is preserved in some areas to a height of nearly 3 m. The two walls terminate at the extreme southwest corner of the plateau in a small, squared room, possibly a low tower or observation platform. This structure has been interpreted as a sentry's station, a possibility furthered by the recovery of 123 small, rounded riverstones, left in a neat pile at the intersection of the walls and the room (fig. 4.32). These stones, apparently sling bullets, were presumably left by someone who intended for them to be readily available, even if they were never used.[84]

The defensive wall turned at a right angle and ran approximately 22 m along the plateau's southern edge before stopping, unfinished, near the remains of the earlier phase's OC2/Workshop. The absence of an eastern-facing return wall would have rendered the building vulnerable to approach from the east, likely indicating the construction of the full defensive work was unfinished at the time of the building's demolition.

Similarly, at the building's northeastern corner, there are the foundations of a projecting feature consisting of two rooms, both slightly larger than the "sentry's house" at the southwest of the plateau. Whether this feature was original to the building's design or added after the original construction of a squared building of four wings, the preserved evidence does not say. However, if this area also served as an elevated platform or watch station, positions to the northeast and southwest would have given defenders a commanding view of the valleys below in every direction except to the west, where the rugged terrain is largely impassable even today.

The construction of wells to the west of Piano del Tesoro at the very end of the site's life suggests a sudden rise in population in this area—new people were likely moving to an area closer to the building, perhaps due to a concern for safety in outlying areas. Moreover, the unfinished construction of defensive works to protect the building itself suggests a growing degree of concern about security among those living within the structure. However, subsequent events would show that these defensive efforts were all for naught.

Indeed, before the southern defensive wall could be completed, the Archaic Phase building was methodically dismantled. Excavation to the west of the plateau revealed the presence of a large depression into which a considerable amount of the building's architectural ornamentation and roof were dumped.

Curiously, some types of ornamentation received special attention in this process. While many gorgon antefixes were found within this deposit, the geospatial distribution of all examples of these antefixes shows that many were simply allowed to fall from the roofline and later were discovered where they fell. Similarly, the distribution of banquet frieze plaques that were not recovered within these deposits to the west of the structure concentrate along the northern flank, while the horse-race plaques are concentrated along the building's western flank. The distribution of the procession scene is less clear but still clusters along the southern flank.

However, the seated and standing figures plaque type was recovered almost exclusively from within this deposition. If the seated and standing figures plaque type ornamented the building's eastern wing, then those individuals engaged in demolishing the building would have been compelled to carry these plaques from the easternmost point on the plateau to the deposition areas at the west of the plateau. It is, of course, appealing to imagine that the reason for this special treatment of the seated and standing figures images related to a specific desire to visually and politically obliterate images of the family it may have represented. Other decorative forms less specifically related to the family's image were treated with a lesser degree of conviction.

Similarly, the seated statues of the building's roofline appear to have been among the very first elements of the building to be removed, and were cast down into the same area. A close reading of the archival documents associated with the trench designated Civitate A24 appears to show an inverse order of deposition, with larger-scale sculpture recovered beneath elements of the building's lateral and raking sima, as well as a number of frieze plaques.

But the seated and standing figures plaques and the human akroteria were not the only materials separated out for a particularly profaning treatment. The two wells excavated to the west of Piano del Tesoro were both intentionally infilled with architectural debris. One well, located approximately 120 m to the west of the Archaic Phase building's western flank, was sealed with hundreds of examples of unornamented roofing tiles, beneath which was a deposit of six ceramic vessels—five oinochoe and one simple bowl—all typologically associated with Archaic period pottery production at Poggio Civitate.[85]

Another well, located only a few meters to the southwest of the

4.33. Well during excavation with sculptural debris

corner of Piano del Tesoro, was similarly sealed. However, unlike the example further to the west, this well was sealed with over
400 kgs of architectural sculpture. Elements of all four frieze plaque
types, nearly intact portions of the lateral sima, and a fragment of at
least one seated human akroterion were all thrown into the well's
aperture (fig. 4.33).[86] However, the first object cast into the well was
not a portion of the building's decorative program. Instead, it was
an ornamental stone platform or altar made of nonlocal travertine
(fig. 4.34).[87] Weighing over 300 kg and standing 0.55 m high, the altar or platform was partially broken and preserves only one corner.
The damage to the object's underside suggests that it was flipped
over and large portions were broken off before it was dragged to the
well and heaved into it.

Large-scale carved or worked stone is exceptionally rare at Poggio Civitate. Areas of non-elite habitation sometimes preserve
examples of a nonlocal *pozzolana* type stone, thought to be associated with grinding grains. In the early years of excavation, a curious carved stone base of unknown function, as well as the base

4.34. Travertine altar and in situ view

of a stele, were recovered within the area of the Archaic Phase building's courtyard.[88] However, beyond these and a limited number of other enigmatic examples of cut or worked stone, only a few stone flakes, beads, weights, and arrow points have been found at the site, some of which may even reflect activities such as hunting that could have preceded the emergence of Poggio Civitate's settlement by a considerable period of time. However, fragments of carved travertine identical to the possible altar were recovered in excavation several years earlier, immediately south of the Archaic Phase building's southern wall. These fragments preserve cut faces and appear to be elements of the lower portion of the original object that had been broken off before they were placed in the well. If so, this may indicate that this unusual stone platform was originally located within the area near or in the southern wing of the building.

In addition to the considerable amount of sculptural debris and the enormous altar fragment that sealed the well, excavation on the open, flat surface outside the well revealed a scattering of debris that included fragments of pottery, small elements of roofing tiles, and bone. Some of these specimens of bone come from an adult human skull.[89] While numerous examples of perinatal human skeletal elements (described above) are found at Poggio Civitate, this is the only example of the physical remains of an adult known from the area of habitation.

Overall, the evidence from Poggio Civitate's final hours suggests the following sequence of events: Elements of the Archaic Phase building's decorative program that specifically depicted images of the site's ruling, elite family were aggressively targeted and removed from the structure. These were taken over to an area west of the building and thrown down into a pit or depression. Other elements of the building's decoration were gathered and thrown into this depression as well, although without the same degree of thoroughness. The altar was broken apart and a large portion of it was dragged over and thrown into a nearby well along with hundreds of fragments of roofing material. Considerable portions of roofing material was carried over to an additional well 120 m west of the plateau and used to seal this additional water source. At some point, at least one individual appears to have been killed in the associated violence. This person's body was left lying on the piazza surrounding one of these wells. The walls of the Archaic Phase building were either knocked over or left to decompose without the protection of the roof.

Excavation over the years has produced a single example of a Roman coin as well as a few fragments of medieval pottery and coins, suggesting the hilltop was occasionally traversed by shepherds or other transient individuals. However, after decades of exploration, nothing suggests Poggio Civitate was ever again a center of sustained habitation.

The Political Situation of the Late Sixth Century BCE

The remarkable circumstances surrounding Poggio Civitate's destruction and abandonment demand the answer to a single question: why? The crude tools of archaeology cannot hope to illuminate the complex social and political motivations for the actions of ancient communities, as these have left no mark in the surviving literary record. However, a broader view of communities throughout the Etruscan world during the years of the mid to late sixth century BCE suggests a degree of political instability and upheaval that may have caught Poggio Civitate in its current.

Evidence from the Etruscan world of the sixth century beyond Poggio Civitate provides a few clues related to this larger conflict. From the city of Vulci, due south of Poggio Civitate, come the remarkable frescoes of the François Tomb.[90] This space's painted ornamentation includes a scene of the semi-historical figures of Macstrna freeing the bound hands of Caile Vipinas as Aulus Vipinas and several figures kill other individuals, some of whom wear *togae pretextae*, togas bordered with purple signifying the elevated, possibly monarchal rank of these men. While not a historical statement, the scene is widely understood as a lost narrative of a violent political interaction between Etruscan, Umbrian, and Latin city-states and the families that dominated them.[91] Moreover, a mid-sixth-century BCE votive dedication at Veii's Portonaccio sanctuary inscribed by Aulus Vipinas, coupled with a comment preserved in a speech given by the Roman emperor Claudius equating *Macstrna* with the legendary Roman king Servius Tullius, suggests complex and sometimes violent political interaction between communities around this time.[92]

The foundation myth of Rome's Tarquin dynasty involves a wealthy family group leaving Tarquinia and taking political advantage of the timely death of the previous king of Rome. While numerous scholars have warned against attributing historical value to these early annalists' narratives, we nevertheless see within the story a movement of elite families between major urban centers, occurring at a point in narrative time earlier, but not overly so, than the supposed events depicted in the François Tomb.

Scholars have implicated the rising city-state of Chiusi in Poggio Civitate's demise.[93] As Chiusi grew in political and economic strength, independent centers of power within its expanding orbit were either absorbed or destroyed. Again, some evidence hints at changes to the social landscape of Chiusi in the mid-sixth century BCE, although we must be cautious when equating archaeological evidence to nebulous historical narratives. Even so, painted chamber tombs of a type very similar to those characteristic of the urban center of Tarquinia appear at Chiusi around the end of the sixth or beginning of the fifth century BCE.[94] The tradition of painting subterranean chamber tombs lasts at Chiusi for only a brief time, perhaps a single generation.

Most scholars commenting on this cluster of Chiusine painted chamber tombs ascribe their presence in this region to a diffusion of fashion from a leading coastal, urban center, Tarquinia. However, this explanation does not fully address the question of why the burial tradition and behavior of a few families around Chiusi suddenly shifted in favor of another community's preferred type of elite burial space. The presence of these Tarquinian-style painted burial chambers at Chiusi may also reflect the presence of a small population of individuals from Tarquinia, relocated to the area around Chiusi. If so, we cannot hope to speculate as to why such families might leave any more than we can speculate why a possible historical analog to the semi-mythological figure Tarquinius Priscus would leave Tarquinia and relocate to Rome at approximately the same point in time. However, it is curious that the same mytho-historical tradition describes how a later member of this dynasty, Tarquinius Superbus, upon his expulsion from Rome, appealed to the military strength of Chiusi and its king, Lars Porsenna, in hopes of restoration.[95] One wonders if this element of the Roman legend of Tarquinius Superbus reflects a familial connection between Chiusi and the Tarquin *gens* established a generation or two earlier.

Given the paucity of actual evidence, we cannot hope to end any discussion of Etruscan or Roman Archaic political history with any sense of certainty. This brief overview is not an indictment of any specific community or family, but rather an attempt to highlight a few points of evidence suggesting that families from some traditional city-states appear to have been involved in intra-Etruscan migration that sometimes took a violent turn. The legendary events depicted in the François Tomb, the various historical myths of elite families moving between communities, and the presence of a generation of Tarquinian-style tombs at Chiusi, all suggest a degree of political instability and social movement throughout the mid to late sixth and the early fifth centuries BCE. Poggio Civitate's demolition and abandonment occur within this same time frame, even as communities such as those in Vescovado di Murlo and elsewhere in the immediate vicinity appear to have continued without obvious disruption. Whoever the specific antagonist may have been, the ultimate demise of Poggio Civitate's leading family within this same period suggests that it was swept up in challenging political times and failed to survive them.

◉ 5 ◉
Poggio Civitate

AN OVERVIEW

Over more than a half-century of exploration of Poggio Civitate, the various interpretations of the site have evolved as the body of collected evidence has grown. Today, it is possible to see, through the considerable archive of data, how the community functioned and thrived in the years between the late eighth and the late sixth century BCE. Moreover, the various chronological phases of elite domestic space preserved at the site provide a remarkable illustration of how such structures evolved in tandem with the social and political needs of the elite families who inhabited them.

In Poggio Civitate's earliest phase of monumental domestic space, reflected in the EPOC4 structure, we see the early antecedents of themes and ideas that continue to find expression in the later stages of the site's political and social development. Revealed in the excavations of the Civitatine area immediately south of Piano del Tesoro, the nonrigid roofing materials employed on structures such as the hut reflect a widely shared tradition of vernacular architecture in existence throughout the central Italic Iron Age. However, the shift to the rigid, tiled terracotta roofing system employed on EPOC4 allowed architects the chance both to radically reenvision the scale of domestic architecture and to employ terracotta as a medium to express concepts and ideas of emerging importance to families interested in promoting the political and economic interests of their progeny by suggesting divine ancestry.

However, the deep, open porch of EPOC4, while allowing for

some degree of communal gathering space, limited the private, restricted areas available to the elite inhabitants of the structure. Moreover, the close proximity of EPOC4 to the smaller domestic structures located to the immediate southwest would have encouraged daily and frequent interaction between aristocratic and non-elite members of the community.[1]

The abandonment of EPOC4 and construction of the Intermediate Phase Complex suggests the increasing degree to which Poggio Civitate's aristocratic family furthered their political narrative of a relationship to divinity. The dramatic escalation of both architectural scale and ornamentation represented by OC Residence, Workshop, and Tripartite building would have required considerable community investment, but resulted in an opulent display of power and authority expressed by the site's leadership. It also resulted in a framing of space between those three structures that limited the visibility of the aristocratic family while providing a large common space where community gatherings could occur in a more controlled environment. This redesign also expanded the community's industrial capacity, providing a working space for laborers from the community engaged in exploiting the area's abundant agricultural and mineralogical resources. This increased production capacity appears to have been largely inwardly directed, with the resulting goods and materials consumed locally and mostly by the ruling family itself, although within a social and ritualized environment that allowed for Poggio Civitate's leaders to redistribute some of these commodities back into the community.

The fire that precipitated the construction of the final, Archaic Phase, building allowed architects and patrons to reimagine once again the nature of elite domestic space. Rather than duplicating the separate structures of the previous phase—each of which had its own function—they instead built a single structure that remains unparalleled elsewhere in the Etruscan world. The building's four wings completely enclosed the space previously flanked by the Intermediate Phase Complex, permitting access to the building's courtyard only through a narrow passageway on the western façade and possibly another on the building's eastern side. This design would have completely obscured the daily activities of the building's inhabitants from view. Moreover, the building's ornamentation similarly suggests a conceptual distinction between exterior and interior space, reflected in the contrasting images of the exterior's gorgon antefixes and the interior's Mistress of Animals appearing on the lateral sima. Regardless of which direction the rooftop akroteria faced, their visibility from either the interior or exterior would have reinforced their purpose: to express the authority of the site's rulers through a connection to a divinely sanctioned—if not actually divine—ancestry.

The scale and visibility of the structure also served another purpose and performed for another audience. On neighboring hilltops visible from Poggio Civitate were other areas of habitation. Poggio Civitate's Archaic Phase building would have been visible to these communities, as it graced the highest hilltop and commanded a view of the valley below. In times of political strife, the people of these communities may have sought refuge within Poggio Civitate's great building, in a manner akin to the way the walled, medieval town of Murlo at times afforded the same protection centuries later. Indeed, such a political strategy may have been essential to marshaling the demographic resources of communities separated by the topography of the immediate area. Unlike the great coastal centers of Cerveteri, Tarquinia, or even an inland community such as Orvieto, where large, elevated, defensible plateaus allow for the aggregation of considerable populations within the same space, the topography of the area straddling the Colline Metallifere and the Crete Senesi did not allow for such population density on a single hilltop. The resulting community lacked a traditional, nuclear center, but enjoyed many of the same benefits of larger, formally urban spaces.[2]

In fact, the town of Murlo, standing adjacent to Poggio Civitate, provides an interesting point of comparison to how Poggio Civitate's Archaic Phase served to provide visual and political cohesion to the broader community.[3] The medieval (and modern) *comune* of Murlo links the multiple communities that ring around it. These

5.1. Comune di Murlo
municipal vehicle

include Vescovado di Murlo, Casciano di Murlo, Lupompesi di Murlo, La Befa di Murlo, and others. Even today, the inhabitants of these various towns share municipal and political resources as well as a common sense of community. Various festivals, banquets, and social events all occur within the *comune*, often within the walled space around the eleventh-century palazzo that originally served as a residence of the Bishop of Siena and now is Poggio Civitate's dedicated museum. Indeed, it is with no small degree of pride that the archaeologists working today at Poggio Civitate note that the modern *comune* has adopted as one of its official symbols the image of the "Cowboy" that once graced the apex of the Archaic Phase building, serving again as a symbol of the unified community below (fig. 5.1).

This possibility may also help explain the curious name of Poggio Civitate, a toponym that, as stated in the introduction to this text, means "Hill of the Cities." This name, derived from Latin and possibly dating to the days when speakers of Rome's language inhabited the area, may capture some distant echo of a collective memory when the hill commanded a collective of communities, bound together by a shared acceptance of leadership emanating from its summit.

We cannot know how Poggio Civitate might have continued to evolve had it not fallen victim to the vicissitudes and violence that marked the declining years of the sixth century BCE. The people who destroyed the site sought not only to render Poggio Civitate uninhabitable by sealing off its access to water, but also to obliterate all visible evidence of the community's political leadership. Embedded in words such as "monumental," "commemoration," and "memorial" is the essential concept of memory. The great structures of Poggio Civitate sought to impress themselves upon the memories of their observers, standing as testament to an august ancestry that lent the community's leaders political and social standing. In tearing down those images, in breaking the sculpture into pieces, in profaning an altar and casting it down into a well, the destroyers of the site sought not only to impose dominion over a defeated community, but to obliterate the memory of its previous rulers. Despite those efforts, through years of excavation and discovery, Poggio Civitate and the communities around it continue to reveal secrets and provide a remarkable window onto life in an Etruscan community during the dynamic early years of central Italy's great Etruscan urban experiment.

NOTES

CHAPTER 1. INTRODUCTION

1. Rowland 1994, 3.
2. Bianchi Bandinelli 1926.
3. Martini et al. 2011, 195–196.
4. Aldinucci and Sandrelli 2004.
5. Note that, throughout the text below, references to materials recovered over the many years of excavation at Poggio Civitate include the excavation's Artifact Identification Number. The prefix PC (for Poggio Civitate, as distinguished from other areas of excavation, such as Vescovado di Murlo, which is prefaced by VdM) is followed by an eight-digit number that is a combination of the four-digit year the catalogued artifact was recovered followed by a four-digit number that records its position in the sequential list of materials catalogued within a year of recovery. For example, the first object entered into the catalogue in 1966 was a fragment of the rim and shoulder of a pithos; its Artifact ID is therefore PC 19660001. Since the early 1990s, the Poggio Civitate Archaeological Excavation Project has sought to digitize the entirety of the excavation's archive. The results of this effort are now publicly available through the archaeological data-sharing platform OpenContext (https://opencontext.org/). To access and explore all related archival information associated with the materials presented here, simply enter a given artifact's eight-digit Artifact ID into the OpenContext system and follow the corresponding links.
6. Campana 2001, 117.
7. Bianchi Bandinelli 1926.
8. Paddock 1993, 176.
9. Phillips 1967, 133.

CHAPTER 2. THE EARLIEST COMMUNITY OF POGGIO CIVITATE

1. In fact, several ceramics recovered from within this midden display strong typological parallels with materials recovered from mid-seventh-century BCE burials excavated on Poggio Aguzzo noted above. For example, see PC 20080002 and compare to Tuck 2009, 109, cat. 25.

2. This deposit is catalogued under the Artifact ID numbers PC 20090092, 20090017, and 20070053.

3. Verhecken (1994, 33) notes that such mollusks are considered a delicacy among modern coastal populations in Spain.

4. Verhecken (1994, 33–34) describes in considerable detail the process of modern replication of this ancient process. The means of production of dyes from these mollusks is described as a "rather disgusting business," suggesting that the area where this work was done would not be considered a higher-status domicile within the larger area of Poggio Civitate's growing community. However, it is equally possible that the concentration of murex was deposited in the midden after the hut's abandonment and not otherwise associated with it.

5. C. Elliott 2008.

6. San Giovenale: Karlsson 2006, 31–36. Roselle: Laviosa 1965 and 1966; Cygielman 2010. One recent study (Winter 2019) suggests a considerably later date for EPOC4, imagining that the construction of the building was never complete and placing its date at the end of the seventh or the beginning of the sixth century BCE. Winter's argument is incorrect on several points. An *oinochoe* (pouring vessel) of uncertain date but possibly produced toward the end of the seventh century was not recovered "below the foundations," nor was a fragment of bucchero similar to specimens associated with OC1/Residence recovered beneath EPOC4's floor. Fortunately, this confusion will be addressed and clarified in the detailed, upcoming publication of this structure that is now in preparation.

7. Phillips 1972, 251. Nielsen 1987, 91. Nielsen and Tuck 2001, 39–41.

8. Considerable debate continues among scholars concerning the date of the development or introduction of tiled roof technology in Etruria. Winter (2009, 55) and then Wikander (2017, 180) focus on the technologies associated with the terracotta roofing systems of Poggio Civitate's Intermediate Phase and prefer a date for the construction of those buildings at or around 630 BCE. However, Wikander is noncommittal as to whether an earlier generation of rectilinear structures, including EPOC4, supported terracotta roofs, although he does appear to accept the possibility that they were designed to do so (Wikander 2017, 218). Damgaard Andersen (2001) is of the opinion that such roofing tiles are present in central Italy at a point considerably earlier than Winter's chronology would allow. Moreover, some elements of the ceramic evidence associated with Poggio

Civitate's Intermediate Phase, to be discussed below, and, setting aside that of the EPOC4 structure, appear to date to the first quarter of the seventh century BCE.

Further complicating this question is the fact that excavation beneath the floor of EPOC4's eastern porch conducted in 2018 and 2019 has revealed cobblestone paving potentially connected to an earlier structure. Resting directly on this surface were examples of flanged terracotta tiles of a form consistent with later pantiles associated with Poggio Civitate's architecture (for example, see PC 20180056 and PC 20190013). While these tiles clearly date from earlier than EPOC4's construction, it is not yet known if they served as roofing elements, or if the paving on which they were recovered was an earlier structure of some form. Several examples of these tiles preserve indications of adhered metal slag, suggesting they were either originally used for metal production or repurposed for this type of production (see PC 20190072). This evidence is currently under study and will be published presently.

9. For example, PC 20150043 (horn akroterion fragment), PC 20150049, and PC 20150066 (both elements of a terracotta plaque depicting a possible quadruped). See Tuck, Glennie et al. 2016 and Tuck 2017.

10. Unfortunately, erosion has damaged this area of the hill and none of these structures preserves a foundation in its entire length. It is therefore impossible to know if these spaces were also designed to have a length divisible by 0.54 m.

11. Tuck 2017.

12. The reuse of roofing tiles from earlier buildings on later constructions is accepted as possible by Wikander (2017, 181). By way of comparison, Quilici and Quilici Gigli (1987, 273) point to examples of the reuse of surviving roof tiles after earthquakes in medieval Italy.

CHAPTER 3. THE LORDS OF PIANO DEL TESORO

1. Bouloumié-Marique 1978.

2. PC 19820174.

3. PC 19820149.

4. Nielsen 1991, 252. Nielsen and Tuck 2001, 37.

5. E.g., PC 19800130. Only eight examples of pantiles from Poggio Civitate display nail holes through their flanges. This number is clearly far too low to justify the conclusion that tiles were secured to rafters with nails. See Wikander 2017, 51–52.

6. Winter 2009, 53.

7. *Case e palazzi*, 70–73. Rystedt 1983; Rystedt 1984.

8. Phillips 1989.

9. Bucchero, typically produced by means of a reducing kiln environment, is

a distinctive, glossy black type of fabric developed in Etruria during the years of the first quarter of the seventh century BCE. See Berkin 2003, 2–5.

10. Boldrini 2000; Boldrini 1994; Phillips 1989, 30–35.

11. For a review of the bibliography and arguments associated with this question, see Tuck and Wallace 2018a, 21, nn. 8 and 12.

12. Tuck and Wallace 2018a, 20–22.

13. Camporeale 1967, 115–116. Tuck and Wallace 2018a, 21–22.

14. Strom 1971, 180.

15. Winter 2009, 51. Wikander 2017, 2018.

16. PC 19710959. Winter 2009, 66. Wikander 2017, 90–91.

17. Winter 1999; Winter 2000; Winter 2009, 72.

18. Nielsen 1987, 94–102.

19. Winter 1977; Winter 2009, 66–67. Wikander 2017, 89.

20. Tuck 2006. The Greek term *potnia theron* is often employed to describe this common type of Etruscan iconography. However, the use of this Greek term should not be taken as an assertion that the Greek and Etruscan expressions of this divinity were entirely equivalent to one another.

21. Damgaard Andersen 1996.

22. Tuck 2010, 216–219.

23. Rystedt 1983.

24. PC 19690284.

25. PC 19680475.

26. PC 19850078.

27. PC 19680554.

28. *Case e palazzi*, 72. Tuck 2010.

29. Tuck 2010, 215–218.

30. Nielsen 1987, 117.

31. Tuck 2010, 217.

32. Rystedt 1984.

33. Phillips 1971, 261.

34. Phillips 1989.

35. Berkin 2003.

36. For example, PC 19710198 and PC 19710280.

37. PC 19710636.

38. Tuck and Wallace 2018a, 73–75.

39. PC 19711017.

40. Tuck and Wallace 2018a, 80–81; Tuck and Wallace 2012a.

41. Maggiani 2006.

42. Tuck and Wallace 2018a, 39–41.

43. Warden 1982.

44. PC 19711015.

45. De Puma 1981.

46. Fibulae are essentially safety pins employed to hold together various forms of garments. They are ubiquitous throughout the region and assume a wide range of forms, from very simple shapes to extraordinarily elaborate ones in a range of metals including most commonly bronze as well as iron, silver, and gold.

47. Warden 1985, 25–45.

48. For example, PC 19710129.

49. Kansa and MacKinnon 2014, 84.

50. Kansa and MacKinnon 2014, 84.

51. See Kalof and Fitzgerald 2003 for a convincing discussion of the interplay between hunting, trophy taking, and male power in modern social contexts.

52. PC 19720523.

53. Steingräber 1985, 329. Tarquinia's Tomba dell'Orco II preserves an image of the god Atia (Hades) wearing a cap fashioned in the form of a wolf's head. See Elliot 1995.

54. Nielsen and Tuck 2001, 41.

55. Nielsen and Tuck 2001, 46–55.

56. PC 19970127. Rasmussen 2006, 114–115.

57. Wallace 2008.

58. Tuck and Wallace 2018a, 19.

59. Cappuccini 2007. Wallace 2008. Tuck and Wallace 2018a, 23–27.

60. PC 19970126.

61. Tuck and Wallace 2018a, 19.

62. Moreover, analysis using a portable XRF carried out in 2017 shows two distinct clay sources associated with PC 19970126 and PC 19970127.

63. This not only suggests that the *Paithnas* gens exchanged ceramics as a totemistic form of political communication, but also hints at intermarriage between communities to further such aims.

64. Tuck and Wallace 2018a, 30–31.

65. PC 19710344 and PC 19720128. Tuck and Wallace 2018a, 29–30.

66. Tuck 1999.

67. Cristofani and Rizzo 1985.

68. Tuck 2006.

69. Nielsen 1998.

70. PC 19850009.

71. PC 19780287.

72. Formigli 1999.

73. Nielsen 1993; Nielsen 1998.

74. Nielsen 1987, 91–92.

75. Tuck 2014, 126. PC 19850151.

76. Winter 2009, 88. PC 19770297.

77. Nielsen 1987, 116. PC 19850033.

78. PC 19840226.

79. PC 19840114.

80. Kansa and McKinnon 2014.

81. Nielsen 1995.

82. PC 19760181. *N.B.*: This example of partially worked antler was recovered from the northern flank of Piano del Tesoro. While it therefore cannot be directly connected with OC2/Workshop, it still clearly shows an aspect of the process of production of materials created at Poggio Civitate.

83. PC 20080011.

84. PC 19790180.

85. PC 19790181.

86. Huntsman and Tuck 2016.

87. This kind of modular construction, especially associated with small carved elements of ivory, is seen in examples of ivory figurines from Marsiliana d'Albegna's Circle of the Ivories burials. See Huntsman and Tuck 2016, 58–59.

88. Gleba 2008, 169–171.

89. Gleba 2012, 3645.

90. Nielsen 1987, 91–93.

91. PC 20090211.

92. Tuck and Wallace 2011.

93. Tuck and Wallace 2011, 201. Tuck and Wallace 2018a, 48.

94. However, this possibility cannot be entirely discounted. Letters or glyphs are occasionally found on rocchetti from other sites. See Bagnasco Gianni 1998.

95. PC 19990053.

96. See Iancu 2018.

97. PC 19950066.

98. Tuck and Wallace 2018a, 99–100. Tuck and Wallace 2018b.

99. Kansa and MacKinnon 2014.

100. Nielsen 1984b. Tuck 2014, 130.

101. Tuck 2006; Tuck 2010.

102. Tuck forthcoming.

103. *Sigla* are small signs or letters placed (usually) in an inconspicuous location on a ceramic or terracotta object. See Bagnasco Gianni and Grummond 2020.

104. Tuck and Wallace 2013, 223–226.

105. Bagnasco Gianni 2014.

106. If these estimates are precisely accurate (and they are likely not, given the incompletely preserved dimensions of the various buildings), the specific weight of the pantiles of OC1/Residence's roof would be 11,968 kg.

107. 15,232 kg.

108. 56,920 kg.

109. Tuck and Wallace 2013, 230–237.

110. Coarelli 1973, 7–31.

111. Tuck 2013.

112. Tuck 2016a, 359.

113. Tuck, Kreindler, and Huntsman 2013, 294.

114. Tuck, Kreindler, and Huntsman 2013, 292.

115. PC 20120200. Tuck, Kreindler, and Huntsman 2013, 299.

116. Tuck, Kreindler, and Huntsman 2013, 300, fig. 16.

117. Tuck, Kreindler, and Huntsman 2013, 302, fig. 20.

118. Tuck, Kreindler, and Huntsman 2013, 302, fig. 21.

119. PC 20130083. Tuck, Kreindler, and Huntsman 2013, 295.

120. Bartoloni et al. 1987. Damgaard Andersen 1993.

121. Campana 2001.

122. Campana 2001, 74–75.

123. Campana 2001, 74.

124. Mangani 1986, 81–82.

125. Tuck, Bauer et al. 2009.

126. Tuck, Bauer et al. 2009, 231–232.

127. Tuck, Glennie et al. 2016, 135–147.

128. Campana 2001.

129. Phillips and Nielsen 1977, 86–87. Tuck forthcoming.

130. *Case e palazzi*, 81–85. Tuck, Glennie, and Kreindler forthcoming.

131. Valentini 1969.

132. Tuck, Wallace et al. 2015, 32.

133. Tuck 2009, 5–10.

134. Gleba 2012.

135. Tuck 2009, 11–23.

136. Harris and Douny 2016.

137. Gauld, Kansa, and Tuck 2018. Trentacoste et al. 2018.

138. Winter 2009, 461. Wikander 2017, 119.

139. PC 19820081.

140. PC 19710017.

CHAPTER 4. MONUMENTAL ASPIRATIONS

1. Donati 1994.

2. Nielsen 1991, 245.

3. Nielsen 1991, 247.

4. Tuck, Glennie et al. 2016, 95.

5. Tuck, Brunk et al. 2010. Tuck, Glennie et al. 2016.

6. Such architectural innovation was known in the region and is seen at Roselle, although this structure might be slightly later in its construction than Poggio Civitate's Archaic Phase building. See Donati 1994.

7. Phillips 1993, 16.

8. Phillips (1972, 251) calls this space a *templum* but refrains from further speculation as to its possible function.

9. Wikander 2017, 126–127.

10. Phillips 1967, 135.

11. Phillips 1971, 258.

12. "Murlo terracotta" typically manifests a Munsell color range between 5YR 6/6 reddish yellow and 5YR 7/1 light gray, although considerable variation results from firing conditions.

13. Phillips 1968, 123.

14. PC 19700129. Phillips 1971, 260.

15. Neils 1976, 5.

16. PC 19680220. Neils 1976, 20.

17. Neils 1976, 20–22. *Case e palazzi*, 116.

18. Damgaard Andersen 1990.

19. *Case e palazzi*, 118–121. Winter 2009, 166–169.

20. Phillips 1974, 267.

21. *Case e palazzi*, 116–118. Winter 2009, 162–163.

22. Newland 1994, 162.

23. Edlund 1992, 178. Since Edlund's publication, seven additional fragments of these types of images have been recovered, indicating that this minimum number should be slightly higher.

24. Edlund 1992, 179.

25. Edlund Gantz 1972. Edlund 1992.

26. Edlund 1992, 184.

27. Frey 2011, 287.

28. Steingräber 1985, 295–296.

29. Edlund 1992, 186.

30. This element of the excavation's history was related to the author by Ingrid Edlund (June 28, 2019).

31. Edlund 1992, 174.

32. PC 19690278.

33. Newland 1994, 12–27.

34. PC 19680635; PC 19680505; PC 19780079; PC 19660259.

35. Root 1973.

36. Phillips (1970, 243) describes these areas as "dumps" associated primarily with the debris of the Archaic Phase building.

37. Small 1971.

38. Gantz 1974.

39. Gantz 1971.

40. MacIntosh 1974, 21–24.

41. Winther 1997, 430–431.

42. Riva 2006, 115. Petersen 2015.

43. Gantz 1974, 6.

44. Steingräber 1985, 283.

45. Antonia Rallo originally made this suggestion in an unpublished paper. De Grummond (2009, 126) also posits this identification.

46. Other forms exist, but the four-spoked version appears to be the more traditional form.

47. Gleba 2008, 173–174.

48. The bibliography related to weaving and women's virtue is considerable; see Foley 1995. Performative weaving in ritual environments, likely intended to reinforce similar social values, is well established in the Etruscan sphere; see Meyers 2013a.

49. Tuck 2021.

50. Bagnasco Gianni and de Grummond 2020.

51. PC 19710684.

52. Tuck and Wallace 2018a, 75–77.

53. On Tomba del Colle, see Steingräber 1985, 266–267. On Tomba della Scimma, see Steingräber 1985, 273–274. On Tomb of the Olympiad, see Steingräber 1985, 328–329.

54. Steingräber 1985, 283.

55. Mangiani 1990.

56. Colonna in Cristofani 1985, 251.

57. Gantz 1971, 9.

58. Llewellynn-Jones 2003, 3.

59. Rathje (1994, 95) states, "The frieze carries a message that may be interpreted as propaganda promoting some of the real people who were connected with the big building at Poggio Civitate." The larger interpretive argument detailed above need not disallow such an interpretation. Indeed, we might envision an intentional blurring of lines between the daily experience of such political propaganda and the episodic replication of such messages through the performance of public, ritual behaviors designed to reinforce social hierarchies within the community.

60. Damgaard Andersen 1996.

61. PC 19690200.

62. PC 19680100.

63. Rystedt 1984, 369–370.

64. Camporeale 1984.

65. Kansa and Tuck forthcoming.

66. Tuck, Glennie, and Kreindler forthcoming suggests a possible connection between the concept of the gorgon and menstruation. If so, the malevolent visage of the gorgon coupled with its representation as a *potnia theron* or Mistress of Animals–style fertility goddess could be a reference to the idea that menstruation represents both a necessary precondition for reproduction while simultaneously indicating the absence of conception.

67. For example, the gesture of the cornetto is made in a depiction of a young dancing girl in Tarquinia's Tomb of the Lionesses; see Steingräber 1985, 316–317. See also Holloway 1986.

68. Damgaard Andersen 1996.

69. Damgaard Andersen 1993.

70. Tuck 2010, 218–219.

71. Not the least of whom are the historical figures Julius Caesar and Augustus Caesar. Julius Caesar's construction of the Temple of Venus Genetrix draws an explicit familial connection between his *gens* and a narrative of descent from Venus through the mythology of Aeneas. Augustus furthers this theme both iconographically, through images that pair him with another child of Venus (Cupid), such as the Prima Porta, and through the patronage of authors such as Virgil, who transform this familial legend into a foundation myth of the city itself.

72. Phillips 1993, 79–83.

73. Cristofani 1975.

74. Edlund-Berry 1994, 16.

75. Turfa and Steinmayer 2002.

76. DeGrummond 1997, 36–38.

77. Meyers 2013b.

78. Phillips 1993, 80–81.

79. *Case e palazzi*, 155–158.

80. Portions of this structure were revealed in 2018 and exploration of it is underway.

81. Phillips 1989, 32.

82. Tuck, Brunk et al. 2010. Tuck, Glennie et al. 2016, 91–108.

83. Tuck, Glennie et al. 2016, 91–94.

84. Nielsen 1991, 246.

85. Tuck, Brunk et al. 2010.

86. Tuck, Glennie et al. 2016, 98–102.

87. PC 20150055.

88. Phillip 1968, 123.

89. Tuck, Glennie et al. 2016, 106–108.

90. Steingräber 1985, 377–378.

91. Coarelli 1983. Holloway 1994.

92. Briquel 1990.
93. Phillips 1993, 80.
94. Steingräber 1985, 266–275.
95. Ridley 2017.

CHAPTER 5. POGGIO CIVITATE

1. Tuck 2017, 239–241.
2. Tuck 2016b.
3. O'Donoghue 2013.

BIBLIOGRAPHY

Aldinucci, M., and F. Sandrelli. 2004. "Geological Framework of the Siena Basin." In *Paleosols: Memory of Ancient Landscapes and Living Bodies of Present Eco-Systems* (excursion guide, Florence 7–11 June 2004), 10–15.

Bagnasco Gianni, G. 1999. "L'acquisizione della scrittura in Etruria: Materiali a confronto per la ricostruzione del quadro storico e culturale." In *Scritture mediterranee tra il IX e il VII secolo a.C. Atti del Seminario 23–24 feb. 1998*, ed. G. Bagnasco Gianni and F. Cordano, 85–106. Milan: Università degli Studi di Milano.

———. 2014. *IESP: The International Etruscan Sigla Project*. Milan. http://etrus cologia.di.unimi.it/index.php/progetti/80-progetti/91-sigle.

Bagnasco Gianni, G., and N. T. de Grummond. 2020. "The International Etruscan Sigla Project: An Introduction." In *Etruscan Literacy in Its Social Context*, ed. R. D. Whitehouse, 113–123. Accordia Specialist Studies on Italy 18. London: Accordia Research Institute.

Bartoloni, G., F. Buranelli, V. d'Atri, and A. De Santis. 1987. *Le urne a capanna rinvenute in Italia*. Tyrrhenica 1. Rome: Bretschneider.

Berkin, J. 2003. *The Orientalizing Bucchero from the Lower Building at Poggio Civitate (Murlo)*. Archaeological Institute of America Monographs, New Series, 6. Philadelphia: University of Pennsylvania Museum of Archaeology and Anthropology.

Bianchi Bandinelli, R. 1926. "Murlo (Siena)—Monumenti archeologici nel territorio." *NSc* 51:165–170.

Boldrini, S. 1994. *Gravisca: Scavi nel santuario greco 4: Le ceramiche ioniche*. Bari: Edipuglia.

———. 2000. "Coppe ioniche e altro: Una produzione occidentale a Gravisca." In *Ceràmiques jònies d'època arcaica: Centres de producció i comercialització al Mediterrani occidental. Actes de La Taula Rodona celebrada a Empúries, els dies*

26 al 28 di maig de 1999, ed. P. Cabrera Bonet and M. Santos Retolaza, 101–110. Barcelona: Museu d'Arqueologia de Catalunya.

Bouloumié, B. 1978. "Nouveaux instruments culinaires (?) en céramique de Murlo (Poggio Civitate)." *MÉFRA* 90: 113–131.

Bouloumié-Marique, A. 1978. "La céramique commune de Murlo (Poggio Civitate)." *MÉFRA* 90: 51–112.

Briquel, D. 1990. "Le témoinage de Claude sur Mastarna/Servius Tullius." *RBPhill* 68: 86–108.

Campana, S. 2001. *Carta archeologica della provincial di Siena* V: *Murlo*. Siena: Nuova Immagine.

Camporeale, G. 1967. *La tomba del Duce*. Monumenti etruschi 1. Florence: Olschki.

———. 1984. *La caccia in Etruria*. Rome: Bretschneider.

Cappuccini, L. 2007. "I kyathoi etruschi di Santa Teresa di Gavorrano e il ceramista dei Paiθina." *RM* 113: 217–238.

Case e palazzi = *Case e palazzi di Etruria*, ed. S. Stopponi (Milan: Regione Toscana, 1985).

Coarelli, F. 1973. *Roma medio repubblicana: Aspetti culturali di Roma e del Lazio nei secoli IV e III a.C.* Rome: Bretschneider.

———. 1983. "Le pitture della Tomba François a Vulci: Una proposta di lettura." *DialArch* 3: 43–69.

Cristofani, M. 1975. "Considerazioni su Poggio Civitate (Murlo, Siena)." *Prospettiva* 1: 9–17.

———, ed. 1985. *Civiltà degli Etruschi*. Milan.

Cristofani, M., and K. M. Phillips. 1971. "Poggio Civitate: Etruscan Letters and Chronological Observations." *StEtr* 39:1–22.

Cristofani, M., and M. A. Rizzo. 1985. "Iscrizioni vascolari dal tumulo III di Cerveteri." *StEtr* 53: 151–159.

Cygielman, M. 2010. "Roselle fra tarde età del Ferro e periodo Orientalizzante." In *Signori di Maremma: Elites etrusche fra Populonia e il Vulcente*, ed. M. Celuzza and G. C. Cianferoni, 55–59. Florence: Polistampa.

Damgaard Andersen, H. 1990. "The Feline Waterspouts of the Lateral Sima from the Upper Building at Poggio Civitate, Murlo." *OpRom* 18: 61–98.

———. 1993. "The Etruscan Ancestral Cult—Its Origin and Development and the Importance of Anthropomorphization." *AnalRom* 21: 7–66.

———. 1996. "The Origin of Potnia Theron in Central Italy." In *Interactions in the Iron Age: Phoenicians, Greeks, and the Indigenous People of the Western Mediterranean*, 73–113. Mainz: von Zabern.

———. 2001. "Thatched or Tiled Roofs from the Early Iron Age to the Archaic Period in Central Italy." In *From Huts to Houses: Transformations of Ancient*

Societies. Proceedings of an International Seminar Organized by the Norwegian and Swedish Institutes in Rome, 21–24 September 1997, ed. J. R. Brandt and L. Karlsson, 245–262. Stockholm: Svenska Institutet i Rom.

De Grummond, N. T. 1997. "Poggio Civitate: A Turning Point." EtrStud 4: 23–40.

———. 2008. "Etruscan Women." In From the Temple and the Tomb: Etruscan Treasures from Tuscany, ed. P. G. Warden, 115–141. Dallas: Meadows Museum.

De Puma, R. 1981. "Etruscan Gold and Silver Jewelry from Poggio Civitate (Murlo)." Archeologia Classica 33: 78–92.

De Puma, R., and J. P. Small. 1994. Murlo and the Etruscans: Art and Society in Ancient Etruria. Madison: University of Wisconsin Press.

Donati, L. 1994. La casa dell'impluvium: architettura etrusca a Roselle. Archaeologica 106. Rome: Bretschneider.

Edlund, I. 1985. "A Terracotta Head from Poggio Civitate (Murlo)." OpRom 15: 47–53.

Edlund-Berry, I. 1992. The Seated and Standing Statue Akroteria from Poggio Civitate (Murlo). Archaeologica 96. Rome: Bretschneider.

———. 1993. "The Murlo Cowboy: Problems of Reconstruction and Interpretation." In Deliciae Fictiles I, 117–121.

———. 1994. "Ritual Destruction of Cities and Sanctuaries: The 'Un-founding' of the Archaic Monumental Building at Poggio Civitate (Murlo)." In De Puma and Small 1994, 16–28.

Edlund Gantz, I. 1972. "The Seated Statue Akroteria from Poggio Civitate (Murlo)." DialArch 6: 167–235.

Elliott, C. 2008. "Purple Pasts: Color Codification in the Ancient World." Law and Social Inquiry 33: 173–194.

Elliott, J. 1995. "The Etruscan Wolfman in Myth and Ritual." EtrStud 2: 17–33.

Foley, H. P. 1995. "Penelope as Moral Agent." In The Distaff Side: Representing the Female in Homer's Odyssey, ed. B. Cohen, 93–115. Oxford: Oxford University Press.

Formigli, E., ed. 1999. I grandi bronzi antichi: Le fonderie e le tecniche di lavorazione dall'età arcaica al Rinascimento. Atti dei Seminari di studi ed esperimenti, Murlo 24–30 luglio 1993 e 1–7 luglio 1995. Siena: Nuova Immagine.

Frey, O. H. 2011. "The World of Situla Art." In The Barbarians of Ancient Europe: Realities and Interactions, ed. L. Bonfante, 282–312. Cambridge: Cambridge University Press.

Fullerton, M. 1982. "The Terracotta Sphinx Akroteria from Poggio Civitate (Murlo)." RM 89: 1–26.

Gantz, T. 1971. "Divine Triads on an Archaic Etruscan Frieze Plaque from Poggio Civitate (Murlo)." StEtr 39:1–12.

———. 1974. "The Procession Frieze from the Etruscan Sanctuary at Poggio Civitate." RM 81: 1–14.

Gauld, S., S. Kansa, and A. Tuck. 2018. "Perinatal Human Remains from Poggio Civitate (Murlo): A Preliminary Presentation." *EtrStud* 21:1–24.

Giannace, M. 2007. "I comprensori indagati del 2005: L'alta valle dell'Ombrone (SI), l'alta val d'Elsa (SI), la val d'Orcia (SI), la bassa val di Cornia (LI), l'alta valle dell'Albegna (GR)." In *Archeologia della vite e del vino in Etruria*, ed. A. Ciacci, P. Rendini, and A. Zifferero, 206–216. Siena: All'Insegna del Giglio.

Gleba, M. 2008. *Textile Production in Pre-Roman Italy*. Oxford: Oxbow.

———. 2012. "From Textiles to Sheep: Investigating Wool Fibre Development in Pre-Roman Italy Using Scanning Electron Microscopy (SEM)." *JAS* 39 (12): 3643–3661.

Harris, S., and L. Douny, eds. 2016. *Wrapping and Unwrapping Material Culture: Archaeological and Anthropological Perspectives*. New York: Routledge.

Holloway, R. R. 1986. "The Bulls in the 'Tomb of the Bulls' at Tarquinia." *AJA* 90: 447–452.

———. 1994. "Cneve Tarchunies Rumach." *Classica: Revista Brasileira de Estudos Clássicos* 7: 101–110.

Huntsman, T., and A. Tuck. 2016. "A Carved Bone Head from Poggio Civitate." *StEtr* 78: 53–59.

Iancu, A. 2018. "Weaving in a Foreign Land: Transmission of Textile Skills through Enslaved Women and through Intermarriages in the Ancient Eastern Mediterranean and Pontus." *Fasciculi Archaeologiae Historicae* 31: 69–79.

Kalof, L., and A. Fitzgerald. 2003. "Reading the Trophy: Exploring the Display of Dead Animals in Hunting Magazines." *Visual Studies* 18: 112–122.

Kansa, S., and M. MacKinnon. 2014. "Etruscan Economics: Forty-Five Years of Faunal Remains from Poggio Civitate." *EtrStud* 17: 63–87.

Kansa, S., and A. Tuck. Forthcoming. "Where the Wild Things Are: New Light on Etruscan Hunting and Trophy Display."

Karlsson, L. 2006. *San Giovenale* 1: *Area F East: Huts and Houses on the Acropolis*. Stockholm: Svenska Institutet i Rom.

Laviosa, C. 1965. "Rusellae: Relazione preliminare della quinta e della sesta campagne di scavi." *StEtr* 33:49–108.

———. 1970. "L'urbanistica delle città arcaiche e le strutture in mattoni crudi di Roselle." In *Studi della città antica* 1. *Atti del convegno di studi sulla città etrusca e italica preromana, Imola 1966*, 209–216. Bologna: Istituto per la Storia di Bologna.

Llewellynn-Jones, L. 2003. *Aphrodite's Tortoise: The Veiled Woman of Ancient Greece*. Swansea.

MacIntosh, J. 1974. "Representations of Furniture on the Frieze Plaques from Poggio Civitate (Murlo)." *RM* 81. 15–40.

Maggiani, A. 2006. "Dinamiche del commercio arcaico: Le tesserae hospitales." *AnnFaina* 13: 317–350.

Mangani, E., ed. 1986. *I centri archeologici della provincial di Siena.* Siena.

———. 1990. "Asciano: Le sculture tardo-orientalizzanti del Tumulo del Molinello." *StEtr* 56: 57–68.

Martini, I., M. Aldinucci, L. M. Foresi, R. Mazzei, and F. Sandrelli. 2011. "Geological Map of the Pliocene Succession of the Northern Siena Basin (Tuscany, Italy)." *Journal of Maps* 7.1:193–205.

Meyers, G. E. 2013a. "Women and the Production of Ceremonial Textiles: A Reevaluation of Ceramic Textile Tools in Etrusco-Italic Sanctuaries." *American Journal of Archaeology* 117: 247–274.

———. 2013b. "Approaching Monumental Architecture: Mechanics and Movement in Archaic Etruscan Palaces." *PBSR* 81: 39–66.

Neils, J. 1976. "The Terracotta Gorgoneia of Poggio Civitate (Murlo)." *RM* 83: 1–29.

Newland, D. 1994. "The Akroterial Sculpture and Architectural Terracottas from Poggio Civitate (Murlo)." PhD diss., Bryn Mawr College.

Nielsen, E. O. 1984a. "Speculations on an Ivory Workshop of the Orientalizing Period." In *Crossroads of the Mediterranean. Papers Delivered at the International Conference Held at Brown University*, ed. T. Hackens, N. D. Holloway, and R. Ross Holloway, 333–348. Archaeologica Transatlantica II. Providence: Brown University.

———. 1984b. "Lotus Chain Plaques." In *Studi di antichità in onore di Guglielmo Maetzke*, ed. M. G. Marzi Costagli and L. Tamagno Perna, 397–399. Rome: Bretschneider.

———. 1987. "Some Preliminary Thoughts on Old and New Terracottas." *OpRom* 16:5: 91–119.

———. 1989. "A New Lateral Sima from Poggio Civitate (Murlo)." In *Secondo Congresso Internazionale Etrusco. Atti Firenze*, 509–515. Rome: Bretschneider.

———. 1991. "Excavations at Poggio Civitate." *StMat* 6: 245–259.

———. 1993. "Further Evidence of Metal Working at Poggio Civitate." In *Antiche officine del bronzo: Materiali, strumenti, tecniche*, ed. E. Formigli, 29–40. Siena: Nuova Immagine.

———. 1995. "Aspetti della produzione artigianale a Poggio Civitate." In *Preziosi in oro: Avorio, osso e corno. Arte e tecniche degli artigiani etruschi. Atti del seminario di studi ed esperimenti, Murlo, 26 settembre–3 ottobre 1992*, ed. E. Formigli, 19–24. Siena: Nuova Immagine.

———. 1998. "Bronze Production at Poggio Civitate." *EtrStud* 5: 95–107.

Nielsen, E., and K. M. Phillips. 1975. "Bryn Mawr College Excavations in Tuscany, 1974." *AJA* 79: 357–366.

———. 1977. "Bryn Mawr College Excavations in Tuscany, 1975." *AJA* 81: 85–100.

Nielsen, E., and A. Tuck. 2001. "An Orientalizing Period Complex at Poggio Civitate (Murlo): A Preliminary View." *EtrStud* 8: 35–64.

————. 2005. "Scavi di Poggio Civitate, 1975–1999: Un breve resoconto." In *Ministero per i Beni e la attività Culturali: La presentazione di attività archeologica*, ed. A Palochini, 843–848. Rome.

————. 2008. "Chronological Implications of Relief Ware Bucchero at Poggio Civitate." *EtrStud* 11: 49–66.

O'Donoghue, E. 2013. "The Mute Statues Speak: The Archaic Period Acroteria from Poggio Civitate (Murlo)." *EJA* 16: 268–288.

Paddock, J. M. 1993. "The Bronze Italian Helmet: The Development of the Cassis from the Last Quarter of the Sixth Century BC to the Third Quarter of the First Century AD." PhD diss., University of London.

Petersen, N. 2015. "The Fan: A Central Italian Elite Utensil." *Tradition: Transmission of Culture in the Ancient World* 14: 301–328.

Phillips, K. M. 1967. "Bryn Mawr College Excavations in Tuscany, 1966." *AJA* 71: 133–139.

————. 1968. "Bryn Mawr College Excavations in Tuscany, 1967." *AJA* 72: 121–124.

————. 1969. "Bryn Mawr College Excavations in Tuscany, 1968." *AJA* 73: 333–339.

————. 1971. "Bryn Mawr College Excavations in Tuscany, 1970." *AJA* 75: 257–261.

————. 1972. "Bryn Mawr College Excavations in Tuscany, 1971." *AJA* 76: 249–255.

————. 1973. "Bryn Mawr College Excavations in Tuscany, 1972." *AJA* 77: 319–326.

————. 1974. "Bryn Mawr College Excavations in Tuscany, 1973." *AJA* 78: 265–278.

————. 1989. "Greek Objects at Poggio Civitate." *AnalRom* 17–18: 29–42.

————. 1993. *In the Hills of Tuscany: Recent Excavations at the Etruscan Site of Poggio Civitate (Murlo, Siena)*. Philadelphia: University of Pennsylvania Museum of Archaeology and Anthropology.

Quilici, L., and S. Quilici Gigli. 1987. *L'abitato di Monte Carbolino*. ArchLaz 8. Rome.

Rasmussen, T. B. 2006. *Bucchero Pottery from Southern Etruria*. Cambridge: Cambridge University Press.

Rathje, A. 1994. "Banquet and Ideology: Some New Considerations about Banqueting at Poggio Civitate." In De Puma and Small 1994, 95–99.

Ridley, R. T. 2017. "Lars Porsenna and the Early Roman Republic." *Antichthon* 51: 33–58.

Riva, C. 2006. "The Orientalizing Period in Etruria: Sophisticated Communities." In *Debating Orientalization: Multidisciplinary Approaches to Change in the Ancient Mediterranean*, ed. C. Riva and N. C. Vella, 110–134. London: Equinox.

Root, M. C. 1973. "An Etruscan Horse Race from Poggio Civitate." *AJA* 77: 121–137.

Rowland, I. 1994. "Early Attestations of the Name 'Poggio Civitate.'" In De Puma and Small 1994, 3–5.

Rystedt, E. 1983. *Acquarossa IV: Early Etruscan Akroteria from Acquarossa and Poggio Civitate (Murlo).* ActRom4 38. Stockholm: Åström.

————. 1984. "Architectural Terracotta as Aristocratic Display: The Case of Seventh-Century Poggio Civitate (Murlo)." *OpRom* 3: 367–375.

Säflund, G. 1993. *Etruscan Imagery: Symbol and Meaning.* Jonsered: Åström.

Small, J. P. 1971. "The Banquet Frieze from Poggio Civitate." *StEtr* 39: 25–61.

Steingräber, S. 1979. *Etruskische Möbel.* Rome: Bretschneider.

————. 1985. *Catalogue Raisonné of Etruscan Wall Painting.* New York: Johnson.

Strøm, I. 1971. *Problems concerning the Origin and Early Development of the Etruscan Orientalizing Style.* Odense: University Press of Southern Denmark.

Trentacoste, A., S. Kansa, A. Tuck, and S. Gauld. 2018. "Out with the Bath Water? Perinatal Human Remains in pre-Roman Zooarchaeological Assemblages." In *From Invisible to Visible: New Data and Methods for the Archaeology of Infant and Child Burials,* ed. Jacopo Tabolli, 133–142. Uppsala: Åstrom.

Tuck, A. 1999. "Wing Handle Cups from Poggio Civitate (Murlo): Ceramic Production and Ceramic Tradition in Inland Etruria during the Orientalizing Period." *EtrStud* 6: 85–108.

————. 2006. "The Social and Political Context of the Seventh-Century Architectural Terracottas from Poggio Civitate (Murlo)." In *Deliciae Fictiles III: Architectural Terracottas in Ancient Italy: New Discoveries and Interpretations,* ed. I. Edlund-Berry, J. F. Kenfield, and G. Greco, 130–135. Oxford: Oxbow.

————. 2009. *Burials from Poggio Aguzzo: The Necropolis of Poggio Civitate (Murlo).* Rome: Bretschneider.

————. 2010. "Mistress and Master: The Politics of Iconography in Pre-Roman Italy." In *The Master of Animals in Old World Iconography,* ed. D. B. Counts and B. Arnold, 211–220. Budapest: Archaeolingua Press.

————. 2014. "Manufacturing at Poggio Civitate: Elite Consumption and Social Organization in the Etruscan Seventh Century." *EtrStud* 17: 121–139.

————. 2015. "2014 Excavations at Poggio Civitate." *EtrStud* 18: 28–40.

————. 2016a. "Scavi a Poggio Civitate e Vescovado di Murlo." *Notiziario della Soprintendenza Archeologia della Toscana* II: 349–362.

————. 2016b. "Poggio Civitate: Community Form in Inland Etruria." In *A Companion to the Etruscans,* ed. S. Bell and A. Carpino, 205–216. Malden: Wiley-Blackwell.

————. 2016c. "The Three Phases of Elite Domestic Space at Poggio Civitate." *Dalla capanna al palazzo: Edilizia abitativa nell'Italia preromana. Atti del XXIII Convegno Internazionale di Studi sulla Storia e l'Archeologia dell'Etruria,* ed. G. Della Fina, 301–317. Rome: Quasar.

————. 2017. "The Evolution and Political Use of Elite Domestic Space at Poggio Civitate." *JRA* 30: 227–243.

————. 2019. "Recent Discoveries at Poggio Civitate (Murlo). *Atti del XXIII Convegno Internazionale di Studi sulla Storia e l'Archeologia dell'Etruria*, ed. G. Della Fina, 497–510. Rome: Quasar.

————. 2021. "Resource and Ritual: Manufacturing and Production at Poggio Civitate." In *Making Cities: Economies of Production and Urbanisation in Mediterranean Europe, 1000–500 BCE. International Symposium, 18–19 May 2017*, ed. M. Gleba.

Tuck, A., J. Bauer, K. Kreindler, T. Huntsman, S. Miller, S. Pancaldo, and C. Powell. 2009. "Center and Periphery in Inland Etruria: Poggio Civitate and the Etruscan Settlement in Vescovado di Murlo." *EtrStud* 12: 215–237.

Tuck, A., J. Brunk, T. Huntsman, and H. Tallman. 2010. "An Archaic Period Well from Poggio Civitate: Thoughts on the Final Destruction of the Site." *EtrStud* 13: 93–104.

Tuck, A., A. Glennie, and K. Kreindler. Forthcoming. "Wine and the Goddess: Drinking Cups, Inebriation, Sexuality, and Politics in the Etruscan Orientalizing Period."

Tuck, A., A. Glennie, K. Kreindler, E. O'Donoghue, and C. Polisini. 2016. "2015 Excavations at Poggio Civitate and Vescovado di Murlo (Provincia di Siena)." *EtrStud* 19: 87–148.

Tuck, A., S. Kansa, K. Kreindler, and E. O'Donoghue. 2017. "2016 Excavations at Poggio Civitate and Vescovado di Murlo." *EtrStud* 20: 35–57.

Tuck, A., K. Kreindler, and T. Huntsman. 2013. "Excavations at Poggio Civitate (Murlo) during the 2012–2013 Seasons: Domestic Architecture and Selected Finds from the Civitate A Property Zone." *EtrStud* 16: 287–306.

Tuck, A., and R. Wallace. 2011. "An Inscribed Rocchetto from Poggio Civitate (Murlo)." *StEtr* 74: 193–202.

————. 2012a. "A 'New' Inscribed Plaque from Poggio Civitate (Murlo)." *EtrStud* 15: 1–17.

————. 2012b. "The Social Context of Proto-Literacy in Central Italy: The Case of Poggio Civitate." *The Accordia Research Papers* 12: 57–68.

————. 2013. "Letters and Non-Alphabetic Characters on Roof Tiles from Poggio Civitate (Murlo)." *EtrStud* 16: 210–262.

————. 2017. "Inscriptions on Locally Produced Ceramic Recovered from Poggio Civitate (Murlo): Literacy and Community." In *Etruskische Sozialgeschichte Revisited, 8–10 Juni 2016. 2. Internationale Tagung der Sektion "Wien-Österreich" des Istituto Nazionale di Studi Etruschi ed Italici. Wien, Austria, June 8–10, 2016*, ed. Petra Amman, 65–73.

————. 2018a. *The Archaeology of Language at Poggio Civitate (Murlo)*. Rome: Bretschneider.

———. 2018b. "An Umbrian Inscription at Poggio Civitate (Murlo)." *Glotta* 94: 273–282.

———. 2018c. "A Third Inscribed Kyathos Fragment from Poggio Civitate." *RM* 124: 301–310.

Tuck, A., R. Wallace, S. Kansa, and C. Horvitz. 2015. *Vinum: Poggio Civitate and the Goddess of Wine*. Massachusetts: Sheridan Press.

Turfa, J. M., and A. G. Steinmayer. 2002. "Interpreting Early Etruscan Structures: The Question of Murlo." *PBSR* 70: 1–28.

Valentini, G. 1969. "Il motivo della potnia theron sui vasi di bucchero." *StEtr* 37: 413–442.

Verhecken, A. 1994. "Experiments with the Dyes from European Purple-Producing Molluscs." *Dyes in History and Archaeology* 12: 32–35.

Wallace, R. E. 2008. "*Muluvanice* Inscriptions at Poggio Civitate (Murlo)." *AJA* 112: 449–458.

Warden, P. 1982. "An Etruscan Bronze Group." *AJA* 86: 233–238.

———. 1985. *The Metal Finds from Poggio Civitate (Murlo), 1966–1978*. Archaeologica 47. Rome: Bretschneider.

Wikander, O. 2017. *Roof-Tiles and Tile-Roofs at Poggio Civitate (Murlo): The Emergence of Central Italic Tile Industry*. Stockholm: Svenska institutet i Rom.

Winter, N. 1977. "Architectural Terracottas with Human Heads from Poggio Civitate (Murlo)." *ArchCl* 29: 17–34.

———. 1999. "New Information concerning the Early Terracotta Roofs of Etruria." In *Proceedings of the XVth International Congress of Classical Archaeology, Amsterdam, July 12–17, 1998*, ed. R. F. Docter and E. M. Moormann, 460–463. Amsterdam: Allard Pierson Museum.

———. 2000. "The Early Roofs of Etruria and Greece." In *Die Ägäis und das westliche Mittelmeer: Beziehungen und Wechselwirkungen 8. bis 5. Jh. v. Chr.*, ed. F. Krinzinger, 251–256. Vienna: Österreichisches Archäologisches Institut.

———. 2009. *Symbols of Wealth and Power: Architectural Terracotta Decoration in Etruria and Central Italy, 640–510 B.C.* Ann Arbor: University of Michigan Press.

———. 2019. "Finding a Home for a Roof in Production within the Building History of Poggio Civitate (Murlo). *EtrStud* 22: 65–94.

Winther, H. C. 1997. "Princely Tombs of the Orientalizing Period in Etruria and Latium Vetus." In *Urbanization in the Mediterranean in the Ninth to Sixth Centuries B.C.*, ed. H. Damgaard Andersen, H. Horsnaes, S. Houby-Nielsen, and A. Rathje, 423–446. Copenhagen: Museum Tusculanum Press.

INDEX

Note: Page numbers in italic type indicate information contained in images or image captions.